Choosing Microsoft Office 365 for the Enterprise

Mini-Book Technology Series – Book 1

Authors: Rand Morimoto, Ph.D., MCSE
&
Guy Yardeni, MCITP, CISSP, MVP

Technical Walkthroughs by: Alex Sandstrom

Cover Photo by: Noble Henderson

DEDICATION

I dedicate this book to my kids Kelly, Noble, Chip,
and Eduardo - Rand Morimoto

I dedicate this book to my wife Allison, she knows why! - Guy Yardeni

ACKNOWLEDGMENTS

We would like to thank the following contributors of thoughts, ideas, and examples that resulted in the content throughout this book:

Alex Sandstrom
Alex J Wong
Brennan Kresser
Eric Trimble
Michael McGill
Nidhi Seth
Rich Dorfman
Subhash Jawahrani
Wally Gallaway

TABLE OF CONTENTS

INTRODUCTION

Office 365 is Microsoft's cloud hosted service that effectively provides Microsoft Exchange, Lync, SharePoint, OneDrive Pro and Yammer on a monthly fee basis. Instead of organizations having to setup, configure, patch, upgrade, update, and backup systems, Microsoft takes care of all of the "backend" server tasks.

Organizations can just focus on being able to access and use applications for email, file sharing, Web conferencing, video conferencing, audio conferencing, document management, and the like.

Users who are already familiar with Microsoft Office continue to use applications like Outlook, Word, Excel, and PowerPoint. In the past several months, Microsoft has updated Office 365 to have full support for non-Windows based systems, so a person running an Apple Mac, or a person who uses an iPad, Android device, iPhone, Windows Surface, or other device can now have the same functionality as users who have traditionally run just Windows.

Office 365 has also evolved in terms of its reliability, security, and the support available for users on Office 365 to be a dependable platform for enterprises to rely on. Office 365 can be said to be a "no brainer" for small businesses as the time, effort, and cost to setup, manage, and maintain a slew of servers costs the organization way more than what Microsoft can provide the hosted Office 365 services to an organization for on a monthly basis.

Mid-size and Large enterprises find Office 365 to be compelling where Microsoft keeps Office 365 up to date on the latest Microsoft server technologies along with ongoing patches and updates. This allows an organization's internal I.T. department to focus on more business critical applications and I.T. services than simply keeping the basics running for email, document sharing, and the like.

End of the day, after several years of fine tuning, Microsoft Office 365 is now enterprise ready in terms of features, functions, security, performance, and reliability, and the content of this book goes through the most common questions and the real world (not marketing speak from Microsoft itself) answers to these questions.

Note: This book is focused to small, medium, and large enterprises as it relates to Office 365 for Businesses and for Enterprises. Many of the

features in Office 365 vary based on the version of Office 365 license purchased, so while this book talks about specific features and functions, it is important to verify that the specific license you are looking to purchase includes the features desired. Microsoft has posted a list of features and comparison of the various versions of Office 365 up on :
http://office.microsoft.com/en-us/business/compare-all-office-365-for-business-plans-FX104051403.aspx?fwLinkID=321496

Additionally, Microsoft from time to time changes the services and limits of their offering, usually INCREASING functionality such as mailbox size limits used to be 10GB per user, that was then increased to 25GB per user, and is now (at the time of the writing of this book (February/2014)) is 50GB per user. However those limits and others do change, the best thing to do is reference Microsoft's Service Description that notes the latest service offerings and limits to service available:
http://technet.microsoft.com/en-us/library/office-365-service-descriptions.aspx

1 IS YOUR ENTERPRISE READY FOR THE CLOUD?

In choosing to host business applications in the cloud, or move existing business application services to the cloud, the enterprise needs to be "ready" for the cloud. An organization that already has key applications in the cloud and is familiar with the cloud is more likely to host other applications in the cloud including key business applications. Likewise, an organization that has had bad experiences with cloud service or where key decision makers are not comfortable with cloud services, it's harder to get those organizations to shift to the cloud.

Understanding Cloud Services

Cloud services come in a variety of offerings. Cloud includes personal consumer services like Facebook or Instagram, or enterprise services like Salesforce.com or Workday. Even within enterprise cloud services, there are a variety of options, whether it's simply email in the cloud, document storage in the cloud, or full line of business applications in the cloud.

The fact that an individual has a negative experience with a personal consumer service doesn't necessarily mean that "all cloud services are potentially bad." In fact, because cloud providers seem to pop up every day, and many of the cloud providers are focused at individual consumer services, a "bad news story" or "bad personal experience" may have no relation to the cloud as a whole. Likewise, a great experience with a consumer service doesn't mean you'll have great experiences with a business-focused cloud service, so cloud experiences have some shared components and some specific to the service offering itself.

Cloud services are also like individual applications and utilities that employees in enterprises have used for years. An employee may have found a great little note taking app, or a great outlining app, but that doesn't mean that the organization will throw away Microsoft Word as the defacto business word processing software for the entire enterprise. There are applications that are core and standard across the enterprise, and those applications that individuals "like" because it does a specific task that suits an individual's need.

It's important for the enterprise to realize the business-wide decisions are not made from the experience of a handful of users on a single utility or applet. The organization needs to choose its enterprise applications with the same responsibility and care that it has for years.

Leveraging Business Critical Services in the Cloud

Business Critical Services are those applications that the organization deems to be most important to the enterprise. Some organizations identify their point of sale and inventory processing system as most critical, especially organizations focused in product orders and shipping logistic transactions. Other organizations have identified e-mail as one of the top business critical service applications in the enterprise. These applications are those that would greatly disrupt the operations of the business if the application were not operational for some period of time.

When choosing to migrate to the cloud, the organization has to choose whether it wants to select a business critical application as their first application to move, and whether that matters. Interestingly, many organization specifically choose a business critical application like e-mail and Web Conferencing communications as their first applications to move to the cloud because the applications are very important to the business, and if someone else can host the applications as reliably (or more reliably) as internal I.T. can do it at a competitive cost, that's one less thing for the organization to spend its cycles managing. Many organizations that have made the decision to move e-mail to the cloud have done so because their business is not running e-mail systems, but rather they are in the business of helping patients, managing mutual funds, producing consumer electronic equipment, and constructing buildings. As such, the focus of I.T. shifts to do things that directly benefit the core focus of the organization.

It's similar to a human resources department that chooses to outsource payroll tax calculation and employee benefits, rather than internally being experts in the intricacies of tax and H.R. laws. The organization can pay a nominal fee to another organization to keep up to date on all the tax and regulation changes, and the contracted organization can also handle the transaction processing.

Financial Decisions Influencing Technology Decisions

For many organizations, the movement to the cloud is a financial decision. Where a fixed monthly payment is better than a capital purchase every few years plus variable ongoing maintenance and support costs of I.T. systems. I usually caution organizations that while the financial decision is one factor, it's not always the factor for choosing what is best for the organization. No doubt if the Chief Financial Officer is the decision maker, and the decision on whether to host IT service in-house or in the cloud is based solely on cost calculations, then no doubt the decision will be financial based.

The key cost factors in choosing a cloud service versus on premise is the cost of hardware, software, security, maintenance, backup, and operational support. These decisions can help an organization identify capital costs as well as operational costs. Some organizations find they save on capital costs, but the ongoing operational costs of help desk support, user training, and general system monitoring remains relatively constant even after moving applications to the cloud. As an example, if an organization has just one I.T. person that takes care of the e-mail system, point of sale system, helpdesk support, etc and the organization moves e-mail to the cloud, it doesn't mean the organization no longer still has point-of-sale support needs, helpdesk needs, or other I.T. support needs.

Cloud Doesn't Solve Fundamental Business Challenges

While a cloud hosted service changes the business model of where an application is run and where data is stored, it doesn't change fundamental business challenges an organization may have regarding user integration with technology systems. As an example, if an organization is struggling over what to do about the security of data on mobile devices in a world of Bring Your Own Device (BYOD) to work, the cloud doesn't somehow fix that security problem. Similarly, if the organization is having a challenge providing help desk support to users working from home, the cloud doesn't solve help desk support challenges.

Cloud hosted services is simply just servers placed in a different location, the day to day application and user support typically does not change one bit in the cloud-hosted model.

Cloud as an Alternative in I.T. Services

The cloud provides an alternative to organizations regarding where the applications are hosted, and may solve problems that are related to an organization running an old or outdated version of software. To address the fundamental business challenges noted in the previous section, while cloud doesn't inherently solve security problems or help desk support problems, many times an upgrade to a new version of software has new features, functions, or simply "works better" and problems of the past go away because of the updated version of software.

For organizations that are several revisions behind on software updates and have a challenge getting around to keeping things up to date, a cloud service may help an organization take the leap to the latest version of an application, and the cloud provider is in the business of keeping the software up to date. This in itself may solve challenges for an organization if keeping current with technologies has been a challenge for the organization in the past.

End of the day though, the cloud is merely an option in I.T. services. The organization can elect to implement technologies in-house, in its own datacenter, or buy services in a hosted environment. The decision is multi-faceted, potentially as a cost saver, and potentially to address ongoing updates.

Leveraging Trial Services to Better Understand a Cloud Offering

To understand how an application works in a hosted cloud environment, organizations can typically setup a trial of the application to get familiar with it. Unlike trying out software on premise that used to typically require setting up servers, loading up software, configuring and integrating systems, and loading up client software, hosted cloud applications typically require minimal setup and configuration efforts. A user can begin testing and trying out an application in the cloud a lot quicker and easier.

That said though, many applications take time to figure them out, or to populate enough data to make the application trial experience helpful. As an example, a client relationship management software experience requires the inputting of client data, lead information, phone call summaries, and other data that can be saved, sorted, searched, and viewed to understand whether an application will "work" for the organization. In these cases, a quick 5 minute evaluation likely is not enough time to get value out of the application, so setting the right expectation to understand the fit for the solution is important.

A good guidance on hands-on evaluations is to jot down a list of "must have" criteria and "important to have" criteria that would be considered "deal killers" if the application didn't do them well, and to put this list together BEFORE even starting the trial. That way the focus of the trial or evaluation is to see whether the application actually does what you "must" be able to do. This will help during the evaluation period to determine whether the trial was a success and whether the application will be valuable to the organization.

Technology Decision Factors: Reliability, Security, Features and Functions?

Also during the evaluation phase, some of the other factors that should be identified are around the reliability of the hosted provider and their financial backing to support the longevity of the application in the cloud. Money is typically the driver for the hosted cloud providers, if they don't make money at what they do, they won't be in business very long, won't be innovative in updating the application frequently, or they may not be able to invest in multiple datacenters and the reliability that the organization needs to have in the running of the hosted application.

Security also comes up regularly whether a hosted cloud provider supports key regulatory compliance factors such as HIPAA, FISMA, European Model Clause, etc as well as whether the content is stored and transported in an encrypted manner. Chapter 4, "How secure and how reliable is Office 365?" covers the security and reliability aspects of Office 365.

And of course, having specific features and functions such as email archiving, or document version controls, or content search are things organizations look to see whether an application meets their needs. However features and functions are a difficult component to use as an evaluation factor because vendors constantly update their products with more features and more functions, so if you wait a few months, the functionality will advance. Again, it usually goes back to the financial funding an organization has to support the ongoing development and expansion of functionality in a product, and the track record the organization has in adding in features and functions. It's less about whether a feature or function is included, but whether the vendor is likely to expand the product with more features, and what the roadmap looks like for future updates.

Microsoft Office 365 – Open for Business and Ready for Enterprises

Microsoft's hosted email and Office in the cloud was released back in 2008 as Business Productivity Online Services (BPOS) based on the "2007" line of products like Exchange 2007 email. BPOS was version 1.0 of Microsoft's business hosted services and a learning model for Microsoft. It was in 2011 that Microsoft released Office 365 based on the "2010" line of products from Microsoft, and the current release of Office 365 is based on the latest "2013" release of their offerings. This is now at least version 3.0 of their offering, and one where Microsoft has figured out how to run a 24x7x365 global datacenter operations in a highly reliable manner. Microsoft, as the developer of the underlying code of Office 365, has focused the code development of the past several years of Exchange, SharePoint, Lync, and Office to be cloud focused.

In 2012, it was still many of the early adopters that were migrating to Office 365, however by 2013, mainstream enterprises started to migrate in mass to Office 365. It's the tipping point where the product is ready, the service is price competitive, and enough organizations have migrated and experienced the service that has now opened the doors for other enterprises to choose to migrate to Office 365 and not feel like they are the "first" or "bleeding edge", but part of the mainstream taking advantage of a trusted and proven cloud hosted service.

Office 365 in the Cloud – More Up to Date then On-Premise Services

Early cloud services typically were a revision or two behind what an organization could implement on premise. However since 2013, Microsoft's Office 365 is now updated before the on premise version of software is made available. Microsoft is truly developing for their cloud first in the case of things like Exchange 2013, where Microsoft is hosting millions of email mailboxes, they are constantly upgrading and updating their cloud software to be reliable and feature rich. The testing process is done in Microsoft's cloud test environment, rolled into Office 365 every 3-6 months, and then released as an on premise update. So organizations today are finding that the cloud version of Exchange Online in Office 365 is actually more up to date than what the organization can implement on premise.

Thoughts and Questions

- Does your enterprise have other cloud-based applications such as Salesforce.com, ADP Payroll, Box.net where the organization is generally comfortable with the performance, reliability, and support of cloud services?
- Do you have a list of "must have" features that you expect from your cloud provider for the apps you are looking to host in the cloud?
- Are there clear business criteria you have in choosing to migrate to the cloud such as key security requirements, financial expectations, problem resolution expectations that are driving your decision to consider migrating to the cloud?

2 WHAT'S IN OFFICE 365

Microsoft's Office 365 is Microsoft's offering for cloud-based email, instant messaging, web conferencing, document sharing, among other core day to day business productivity tools. For those familiar with the Microsoft server line of products, it is effectively Microsoft's latest Exchange, SharePoint, and Lync in the cloud. Users have full access to the functionality of these server system services, but the I.T. organization does not have to patch, update, or maintain the backend servers. Instead, the organization just pays a monthly fee for the use of the service.

Exchange Online in Office 365

The main component of Office 365 that organizations implement and utilize is the email component of Office 365, also commonly referred to as the Exchange Online component of Office 365. The email function in Office 365 is effectively the latest Exchange 2013 server product that is hosted by Microsoft. Everything that a user normally has in connecting their Microsoft Outlook client to Microsoft Exchange is included such as email, calendaring, contacts, tasks, and the like.

Email is frequently identified as one of the top mission critical applications an organization has, and there are two camps to hosting email in the cloud. Some organizations feel that email is so critical, that the organization HAS to keep the email on premise and manage it themselves. The other side of the spectrum are organizations that also feel email is mission critical, and so much so, they need to get it out of their own datacenter, put it in the hands of someone like Microsoft that is hosting millions of other mailboxes, so that the organization can focus on other things that are critical to the organization such as the enterprise's Time and Billing system, or ERP system, or the like.

Standard Microsoft Outlook Client Connected to Office 365

Regardless of which camp you are in, email is email, it's nothing more than typically content-based messages that occasionally has an attachment or two that is sent between users. Email for the most part hasn't changed in the past couple decades, and has proven to be a very common application that organizations are moving to the hosted cloud environment because of the importance of email, and the success organizations like Microsoft has in hosting the application in the cloud.

Utilizing Basic Email Messaging Services in Office 365

Email in Office 365, being nothing more than Exchange 2013 in the cloud, provides users the EXACT functionality as if they were accessing Exchange 2013 in their own datacenter. The features and functions are identical. The user can access their emails from the Outlook client that they've been using for years. The user can access email from their mobile phones as well as from an Outlook Web App (OWA) Web-based application.

With identical functionality, users switching from an on premise experience to the hosted Office 365 email experience typically don't notice any differences, unless of course they are migrating from a much older version of Exchange, then the users actually might find significantly better support for mobile devices, Apple Macs, and even better functionality from the latest Windows-based client software.

The key is that the users get more than less, and the look and feel remains the same for the users, thus the migration to Office 365 for email is a relatively uneventful migration as far as the users are concerned.

Calendaring Across the Enterprise

Office 365 not only provides email functionality that is identical to what users have used for years in Outlook, but also calendaring remains the same. The calendar functions in Office 365 are the built-in calendaring of Exchange 2013. During a migration, all calendar appointments from Exchange are migrated across including calendar delegates, recurring appointments, notes, and settings. Users familiar with Microsoft Outlook for calendaring won't notice any changes, and everything will continue to work in the same manner.

Many organizations have looked to Office 365 for calendaring as a solution to resolve calendar corruption, delegation problems, and the like that the organization has experienced with calendaring in their on premise Exchange environment. Couple things on the resolution of calendaring issues in Office 365. First of all, if the calendar corruption issues being experienced have been caused by the organization using an old version of Microsoft Exchange, or one with known problems with calendaring corruptions, then a migration to Office 365, which is built on the LATEST release of Exchange, could very likely resolve the calendaring corruption problems the organization has been experiencing. However the second reason calendars get corrupt is because endpoints being used for calendar delegation are cross platform, where an executive might be using Outlook 2011 on a Mac system, but the executive administrator managing the calendars is running on Outlook 2010 for Windows. Many times with calendar corruption, the problem lies in the mixed endpoint modifications that occurs. By migrating calendars to Office 365, yet still using a mix of Windows, Macs, iPads, and Android devices to directly access, manage, and administer calendars likely won't resolve the calendaring problems. So some problems may be addressed because of the latest release of Exchange that Office 365 provides that has addressed many calendaring corruption issues, and endpoint configurations that likely won't change just from a cutover to Office 365 and thus won't be a solution to the problem.

Utilizing Personal and Shared Contacts

Contacts, or the Address Book, is another core function used by Microsoft Outlook users. Users typically have the corporate contacts, sitting in what Microsoft has called the "Global Address List", or GAL, for years. The GAL includes all of the names and contact info of users with email boxes in Exchange today. The GAL pulls from the organization's Active Directory list.

Users also have personal contacts, names and information that they have saved to their Outlook or synchronized mobile phone over the years. These personal and shared contacts are migrated over to Office 365 and accessed by the user exactly as they have used in the past, either displayed when the user clicks the "To" or the "CC" in an email or searches for a contact on their endpoint client system.

Leveraging Lync Online in Office 365

Once users migrate their old emails, calendar appointments, and contacts to Office 365 and email is working as expected, organizations look to enable the Lync Online component of Office 365. In the Microsoft ecosystem, this is effectively Lync 2013 in the cloud. Lync provides instant message, Web conferencing, person to person video conferencing, and person to person audio conferencing.

Lync Online ties into the Exchange Online component in Office 365, thus Lync contacts are nothing more than personal and shared contacts in the address book. Many organizations that are using various Web Conferencing services like WebEx, GoToMeeting, or the like consider getting rid of their old Web Conferencing service and just utilize what Microsoft includes as part of Office 365. Feature for feature, organizations find that what Microsoft provides for Web Conferencing is the same as what they are paying another vendor for, so they might as well save money, simplify functionality, and use what is included in the cost of Office 365.

Chapter 12, "What's Lync like in office 365?" covers more details on Lync in Office 365.

Using Instant Messaging in Lync Online

Lync Online in Office 365 includes instant messaging, where users can carry on real time chats with others. And with Office 365, instant messaging is not only between users within the organization, but through the click of an enterprisewide configuration setting users are allowed to carry on instant messaging conversations with users outside the organization.

Lync Online's federation of connecting organizations to other organizations over instant messaging extends IM conversations to users of other Office 365 environments, to users who have Lync on premise, as well as IM conversions with IM users on Skype, Yahoo! Messenger, and Microsoft Live Messenger.

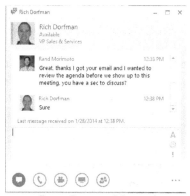

Lync Instant Messaging

Centralizing on Lync Online's Web Conferencing Functionality

With built-in Web Conferencing in Lync Online, organizations can do person to person Web meetings, as well as invite upwards of 250 users to a conference to be able to share presentation materials, share a desktop, and share an online digital whiteboard. Many organizations that had Lync on premise may have still used an external cloud-hosted Web Conferencing provider like WebEx or GoToMeeting so that the organization did not have to setup the scale of servers and allocate the needed network bandwidth to host large meetings with clients and external users. However since Lync Online in Office 365 is already a hosted service, organizations can now just consolidate their Web Conferencing functions into Lync in the cloud.

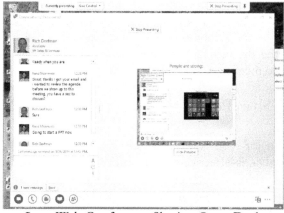

Lync Web Conference Sharing Out a Desktop

Another blocker that many organizations previously found with early versions of Microsoft's Lync Web Conferencing was Microsoft's lack of support or limited support for non-Windows based endpoints. However in the past year, Microsoft has expanded support to non-Microsoft endpoints with full Web Conferencing support for Apple Mac users, a Lync client for iPads, iPhones, and Android devices, as well as a full featured browser client for Lync meeting communications. So the limitations that previously existed in Microsoft's Lync for enterprise Web Conferencing has been addressed in Lync in Office 365.

Lync to Lync Voice Communications in Lync Online

Lync also provides person to person voice communications, either within a Web Conference with internal and external participants, or the Lync to Lync voice communications can be established directly as a user to user audio call. Using a headset, handset, or speaker on a system, voice communications can be established between Lync users, and the conversations can be multi-way to include dozens of voice participants on the same call.

Lync to Lync Video Communications in Lync Online

Beyond just voice conversations, Lync also provides the ability for video conversations in the same call or Web Conference. As long as a system has a camera attached to it, the video can be activated and users can now participate in video conversations. With Lync, the existing voice conversation does not need to be dropped and replaced by a video conversation, instead, the existing voice conversation can have the video ADDED to the same conversation. And not all participates need a camera, just the person who wants to turn on the camera and share video during the conversation, so potentially a camera on the main presenter of a session, or a room based camera to do video between rooms of individuals.

Lync provides the ability to extend the dimensions of conversations and meetings on the fly, turning a simple call into a video call, or turning an audio and video meeting into a full blown Web conference.

Choosing SharePoint Online Versus SharePoint On-Premise

Another major component in Office 365 is SharePoint Online. SharePoint Online is effectively Microsoft's SharePoint 2013 in the cloud. SharePoint provides document library storage, content version control, workflow approval of content, and collaboration of information. SharePoint has been broadly adopted in enterprises in the on premise releases of SharePoint 2007, 2010, and 2013, and more recently organizations that have Office 365 have been leveraging SharePoint Online for new functionality, and migrating on premise content into the cloud-based version of SharePoint.

Earlier releases of SharePoint in Office 365 (and BPOS before it) were drastically limited in what an organization could do with the cloud-based version of SharePoint, and as such, SharePoint Online was not used much in early implementations of Office 365. Organizations may have moved their email and calendars to Office 365, but kept SharePoint on premise. However SharePoint in the latest Office 365 now provides similar functionality as SharePoint 2013 provides on premise, and with comparable features and better customization flexibility, organizations can leverage SharePoint Online more.

Additional information on SharePoint in Office 365 is covered in Chapter 14, "Are organizations really using SharePoint Online?"

Document and Media Libraries in SharePoint Online

One of the main things organizations use SharePoint for is for the document and media library capabilities of the product. SharePoint allows the creation of document storage areas, or libraries, where content can be saved, posted, and shared. The content does not need to be simply word processing documents and spreadsheets, but could also include video files, audio files, pictures and graphic files, and other rich media content. Content within SharePoint libraries can be flagged to be shared with others both inside the organization and to a limited manner shared with those external to the organization.

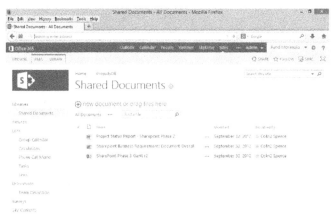

SharePoint Document Library for Sharing Content

Version Control to Manage Documents

Content within a SharePoint document library can be enabled for version control management. Any time someone makes changes to content, a version tag is updated so that users will know which version of the file is the most current version. Organizations commonly use the version controlling feature for Microsoft Word documents where previous versions can be compared from one to another to see what was modified and edited, as well as when content is updated, comments can be added to the document posting the purpose of the change as well as tag the document as being an approved as the final version of a document.

Workflows Assisting Enterprise Communications

Within enterprises, beyond just posting content and performing version controls on the content, the ability to route documents to a group of users for review and approval becomes an important process task. As an example, a policy document that gets written rarely goes straight from the author and right out to the organization as a formal policy. Frequently a group or committee would review the policy change, and would edit, comment, and make changes to the content. Reviewed content then goes through grammar edits and general content clean-up. After a draft document is approved by a committee and properly edited, the content typically gets reviewed and approved by the legal department or human resources department before being published.

SharePoint Online provides workflow capabilities that helps enterprises build approval routes, and then takes content and applies the approval route to the content, gets electronic approvals, and ultimately gets posted.

OneDrive Pro as a Personal and Shared File Repository

OneDrive Pro was recently added to Office 365 for enterprises to be able to allow users to store personal content as well as allow users are able to share content with others. As was noted in the section "Document and Media Libraries in SharePoint Online," SharePoint content can be stored in SharePoint document libraries, but for the most part, SharePoint content is focused at workgroups or across the entire enterprise. Users still need a place to store their own personal content.

With OneDrive Pro in Office 365, a user can upload personal content, potentially personally written documents and memos, could be photos and other content that the user may have previously stored in their "My Documents" folder on their system. However unlike "My Documents", OneDrive Pro content is accessible from the Internet, not just to the "My Documents" folder on the local hard drive that the user was working from.

Additionally, OneDrive Pro content can be shared with external users, something that enables users the ability to collaborate with others, and for enterprises, hopefully the ability to minimize the use of other 3rd party file sharing tools at an additional expense, like the use of Box.net, Dropbox, and the like.

Yammer – Enterprise Social Networks

Yammer is the newest addition to the Office 365 family of services. Yammer is a cloud-hosted social media provider that effectively provides even better collaboration and communications capabilities beyond what an organization could have done in the past with just SharePoint. As much as SharePoint provides some level of collaboration and workgroup communications, Yammer was built as a collaboration and workgroup communications tool from the ground up. Yammer has from the beginning been solely a cloud-based tool, as such, it provides organizations the ability to communicate not only within the office, but when workgroups span multiple offices, on the road, from home, or from anywhere. Additionally, Yammer was not always a Microsoft solution, and has broad support for endpoints including Apple Macs, iPads, Android devices, and the like.

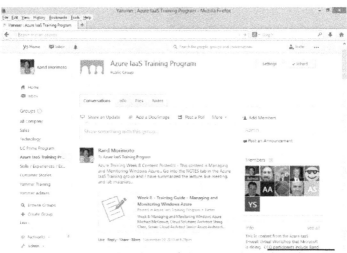

Yammer Posting and Conversation Thread

Organizations use Yammer to post content and messages, share files, make workgroup or companywide announcements, and invoke responses from feedback from others in the organization. For many organizations, Yammer has replaced group email messages, being that emails and email replies are subject to a send and reply of a single thread. Also with emails, users who were not included in the email do not have access to the shared information. Yammer provides a post and reply threaded view of conversations so that someone can come back days later and catch up on the conversations and discussions that occurred while they were away. Or users can search the thread of conversations to look up information, similar to searching a mailbox, but across multiple conversation threads.

Yammer has replaced "public folders" in Exchange for many organizations, where content was posted and shared with others. And while Microsoft continues to support public folders in Office 365 for email conversations, Yammer not only provides the ability to post content, but the ability to collaborate more real time to the content threads of information.

More on Yammer is covered in Chapter 16, "What the Heck is Yammer?"

Microsoft Office for Windows and Mac

Lastly, in Office 365, Microsoft provides subscriptions to the Office 365 service that includes a license for Microsoft Office for Windows and for Macs to help organizations consolidate their licensing of products. With Office included in the licensing, Microsoft also provides Web based views and editing of documents, spreadsheets, and content so that a user doesn't even need to install a copy of Office on their desktop, laptop, tablet, or endpoint system. The user can view a Word document and edit the document real time within Office 365. The most common features of Microsoft Office are included in the Office Web Apps, and greatly simplifies content management and access.

Add-on Subscriptions to Office 365

Microsoft offers a number of add-on subscription items to Office 365 beyond the basics of Word, Excel, PowerPoint, Outlook, OneDrive, and Yammer. Organizations can add on subscriptions for Microsoft Project, Microsoft Visio, and Microsoft Dynamics CRM. These are all available to be added to an organization's subscription to add functionality to user's day to day business productivity interactions.

Thoughts and Questions

- Most organizations start with leveraging the email and calendaring functions of Office 365. Does that make sense for your enterprise and its use of Office 365?
- Where does Web Conferencing fit in for your enterprise? Will consolidating Web Conferencing services to what Lync Online provides save the organization in current expenses for Conferencing services?

- Is file sharing and document collaboration in use in the enterprise, and will the SharePoint Online capabilities of Office 365 be of benefit to the enterprise?
- Does your organization have a need to collaborate internal and external to the organization where something like Yammer within Office 365 may help in the distribution, sharing, and feedback in communications?

Is the make-up of endpoints in your enterprise now or potentially in the future a mix of Windows, Macs, iPads, iPhones, and Android devices where multi-platform support of Office 365 can help the organization in the mixed endpoint environment?

3 IS IT REALLY EXCHANGE 2013, BUT IN THE CLOUD?

As migrating email to Office 365 is usually the impetus for organizations to migrate to Office 365, the big question is whether Office 365's email is really just Microsoft Exchange 2013 in the cloud. The answer is a definite Yes. While the earlier releases of Office 365 were lacking features and functions found in the on premise version of Exchange, most recently, the feature set between Office 365 and Exchange 2013 on premise is now the same.

Identical Experience for Outlook 2013 / Exchange 2013 On-Premise Users

As far as users are concerned, their access to Outlook and Exchange functionality is the same when connecting to Office 365 as they had if they were connecting to Exchange 2013 on premise. Office 365 supports the Microsoft Outlook 2007 (or more current) client for Windows users, and the Microsoft Outlook 2011 for Mac client (or more current) for Mac users. For users who have been using Outlook 2013 against an Exchange 2013 environment previously, and now will be using the same Outlook 2013 client against Office 365, those users would likely not even know they were migrated.

All of the functionality in Outlook 2013 continues to operate in the same manner as before. The user can create emails, create meeting appointments, search contacts, setup inbox rules, categorize messages, etc.

Similar Experience for Users of Earlier Versions of Outlook and Exchange

Even for users who were previously running an earlier version of Outlook (i.e.: Outlook 2010 or Outlook 2007) against an earlier version of Exchange (i.e.: Exchange 2003, 2007, 2010) would find their experience to be similar to what they had prior to the migration to Office 365. Say for example if a user used to run a version of Outlook 2010 and continues to use the Outlook 2010 client against Office 365, their experience and usage of the Outlook 2010 client would not change after the migration to Office 365.

Obviously if a user was familiar with the Outlook 2007 client and the organization during the process of migrating to Office 365 also migrated users to the Outlook 2013 client, then the user would experience a change, not because of the migration to Office 365, but because of the change from Outlook 2007 to Outlook 2013. So the user experience is for the most part tied to the client software they are running, and not necessarily the fact that their email was migrated to Office 365.

Experience for Non-Exchange Migrated Users

Similar to the experience for users of earlier versions of Outlook migrating to Office 365, the experience of the non-Exchange migrated user is tied to the client software they are familiar with. This would apply to users of Gmail, GroupWise, Lotus Notes, etc. If the user was using Outlook 2010 against Gmail and switches to Office 365, if they continue to use Outlook 2010, their functionality would be similar in terms of creating email messages, calendar appointments, and the like because their previous email experience would have been with the Outlook client. However for a user that has used the GroupWise client as their sole email client that then migrates to the Outlook client, there will be an experience change for the user. We do find that while an organization migrating from something with a different client software like the GroupWise client or Lotus Notes client may be shifting users to the Outlook client, because Outlook has been so dominant in the email marketplace, users have frequently used Outlook at some point in their career and are familiar with how Outlook works.

Outlook Web App Experience for Office 365 Users

One of the big improvements in Exchange 2013 that is rolled into Office 365 is Outlook Web App (OWA) that works on all modern browsers on all major operating systems with the exact look and feel across platforms. Users are no longer subjected to a "lite version" that has limited functionality on one device versus another. Microsoft has standardized on an HTML5 standard, as such, the functionality, user interface, and operations is the same across browsers.

OWA is also the same when accessing email, calendars, and contacts from a tablet or mobile phone. Again, with a current browser that supports HTML5, a user can sit on an iPad or an Android phone or other form factor endpoint and experience similar functionality. Microsoft has an auto-sizing capability where OWA detects the form factor of the device, and for a full screen system, will display what Microsoft calls a 3-wide format that includes the navigation window on the left, the message window in the middle, and the preview window to the right.

Side by Side – Outlook for Windows and Outlook Web App
Similar Visual Experience

On a tablet, the user would see a 2-wide format that includes messages and the message preview. And on a small phone screen, the user would see a 1-wide format that includes just a list of messages with no displayed navigation bar or preview. The display is optimized to the form factor of the device, and to navigate between folders, the user can still click a navigation button that will provide them a list of the various folders in their mailbox.

All of the Functionality, but None of the Server Maintenance and Update Responsibilities

With Office 365, users have for the most part used the Outlook client or are actively using the Outlook client and their access to features and functions in Office 365 does not change, or if anything, improves their experience with added functionality. While retaining a similar user experience with Office 365, the key to Office 365 is the organization no longer has to do server and database maintenance! All of the daily, weekly, monthly maintenance requirements of Exchange that included backing up emails, restoring emails, patching servers, installing interim updates, performing major upgrades, recovering from corrupt mailboxes and databases, all of those Exchange administrator tasks are no longer the responsibility of the internal I.T. department.

Familiar Exchange Administration for Exchange 2013 Administrators

For Exchange Administrators, as much as there are no "backend" maintenance responsibilities of patching, updating, and backing up the servers, the administrators do have FULL access to all other administrative tasks. For administrators who have previously managed an Exchange 2013 environment, the exact same Exchange Administration Console (EAC) is used. Within the EAC, the administrator can perform tasks including Adding mailboxes, Deleting mailboxes, disabling mailboxes, creating inbound and outbound SMTP routes, creating and checking spam filters, searching for lost messages that might have been caught in quarantine, performing e-Discovery content search tasks, creating distribution lists, managing public folders, etc.

Effectively everything that is done by an Exchange 2013 administrator in the EAC is available to the Office 365 Exchange Administrator. In a Hybrid mode where an organization has some mailboxes on premise in an on premise Exchange server and some users in Office 365, the organization will have at a minimum an Exchange Client Access Server (CAS) and Mailbox Server (MBX) on premise and can use the old Exchange Management Console on premise to manage tasks like managing mailboxes, enabling POP or IMAP functions, disabling mobile devices, etc.

Additionally, PowerShell remains available to perform all of the same tasks for creating and deleting mailboxes, archiving mailboxes, etc that has been available in the past. Microsoft provides a remote PowerShell capability to Office 365 to perform PowerShell based tasks.

The only things that the Exchange Administrator won't have access to would be creating Exchange databases, creating cloud-based CAS or Mailbox servers, managing Database Availability Groups (DAGs) or other "server-based" and "high availability based" server functions in Office 365. Those are obviously relegated to Microsoft's Office 365 team and not something that the Exchange administrator needs to deal with anymore.

Better Administration Experience for Exchange 2010 or Earlier Administrators

For users of earlier versions of Exchange such as Exchange 2010, 2007, 2003, the management interface will be different for the administrator if the administrator say for example has been used to using the old Exchange 2003 Administrator tool, or the old Exchange 2007 Management console.

However all of the Office 365 administration tasks are available in a Web based graphical user interface with drag and drop as well as right-click functionality within the interface, so the administrator can quickly figure out how to add, modify, and delete settings.

In fact, many administrators of old Exchange environments find the Office 365 administration functions easier because in the past the administrator likely had to do some tasks in the Active Directory Users and Computers console and some tasks in the Exchange Management Console and potentially even other tasks in the separate Public Folders console. With Office 365 (as with Exchange 2013), all of the core functionality from creating mailboxes, adding additional email addresses to users, adding a user to a distribution list, and managing public folders is in the same Exchange Administration Center.

Thoughts and Questions

- Are your users using Outlook 2013 now, if so, their experience in Office 365 will be the same once they are migrated to Office 365?

- Will your users continue to use the same Outlook client as they have today after the (initial) migration to Office 365, if so, their experience in Office 365 will be the same?

- Would your users like the same full feature rich functionality of Outlook Web App (OWA) regardless of which modern browser or endpoint operating system they are running today?

- Have you administered Exchange 2013 previously? If so, you will find the same functionality available for Exchange administration in Office 365 as you've had in the past.

- If you've administered earlier versions of Exchange, you will find the user interface will be the new Exchange Administration Console, however all of the day to day functions are available for you to use.

- If you plan to do an Office 365 trial, as an administrator, take a look at the Exchange Administration functions, you should find all of the features and functions you need to perform your day to day tasks available to you.

4 HOW SECURE AND HOW RELIABLE IS OFFICE 365?

As many organizations identify email and calendaring as one of their top mission critical applications, when choosing to migrate to Office 365, undoubtedly the question about security and reliability of Office 365 comes up. While a year or two ago I might have responded that the reliability was "good", Microsoft, like most of the early cloud hosted providers were going through learning and growing pains with their cloud services and experienced interruptions in service every few months for a subset of users. However since about 2013, Microsoft has gotten the uptime thing figured out, and they share uptime data which ranges from 99.94 to 99.97% uptime for the past several months from the writing of this book (Feb/2014).

Office 365 Uptime Compared to Most Enterprises

In looking at uptime in the Office 365 environment, Microsoft has been able to achieve 99.95% range of uptime on email which is actually better than most enterprises because Microsoft has NO regularly scheduled maintenance windows on their environment. You won't get a message from Microsoft that they are doing "maintenance this weekend with a 2-4 hour outage window", that does not happen. Microsoft does rolling patches and updates of their environment so that mail is failed over between server nodes in their datacenter to fully patched and updated end systems. Thus, for the normal business enterprise running Exchange in-house that brings their email system down or reboots their system monthly or quarterly, that downtime is not experienced in Office 365.

While it has been a long while since I've heard any of our customers experiencing an outage with Office 365, when Microsoft has service interruption, it might be on a specific node in one of their many datacenters around the world hosting mail and is limited to a specific group of users. So outages are isolated to blocks of users, unless a catastrophic datacenter event occurs, which again, as of the time of the writing of this book, a major event in an entire datacenter has never occurred with Office 365.

Regional Datacenter Clusters

Architecturally, Microsoft hosts Office 365 data in datacenter clusters, which they have a datacenter cluster in North America consisting of 4 datacenters across the region, a datacenter cluster in Europe consisting of 3 datacenters across the region, and a datacenter cluster in Asia consisting of datacenters across Asia. Mail is geographically redundant across a regional cluster of servers so that at any time, an organization's mail may be in one datacenter in a region or another datacenter in a region. Microsoft, at their choosing, replicates the content and fails over content between the datacenters in the region to perform database, server, and site upgrades and updates, keeping in mind their 99.9% insurance backed uptime commitment in the process.

Microsoft does not failover datacenters across continental regions at this time, primarily because regulatory standards of hosting data for example of European Union citizens in the United States is subject to compliance limitations, as such, Microsoft keeps regional data within a region.

Dashboard to See Uptime Status

At any time, an Office 365 administrator can go to their Office 365 portal and view the uptime status of all Office 365 services including current and historical status. Many times users might hear on the news that there is a "Microsoft service outage" and the administrator can verify if their organization may be impacted.

Office 365 Service Health Dashboard

Many times outages reported on the news are related to other Microsoft cloud services like the Azure network, or Xbox gaming network, or the like and not Office 365, so it is handy for an administrator to be able to jump online and check the status of their Office 365 services.

Security – Defense in Depth

As for security of Office 365, Microsoft has their entire Microsoft Trust Center where they publish their security standards, and how they address regulatory compliance and privacy protection. (http://office.microsoft.com/en-us/business/office-365-trust-center-cloud-computing-security-FX103030390.aspx) Effectively, Microsoft has in place for their Office 365 offerings a comprehensive Defense in Depth security strategy.

Starting with physical security, Microsoft doesn't provide tours of their Office 365 datacenters to the public and has very stringent practices leveraging biometric access controls to log everyone who enters and exits their datacenters. Suffice to say, Microsoft's physical security far exceeds the "computer closet" of most small businesses and even the standards for access of most enterprise businesses with the logging, tracking, background checks, and other processes required to be permitted to enter a Microsoft datacenter facility.

Beyond physical security, Microsoft leverages security best practices for connectivity to the Internet that includes no remote access into the servers and systems that host Office 365, intrusion detection devices along with the latest in anti-malware protection not only for an organization's email messages, but for the core operating systems that Office 365 is built on.

Flipping around from the datacenter side to the Office 365 user side, Office 365 content is accessed by users through SSL-based encrypted sessions, whether it's requiring HTTPS to access content in Outlook Web App, SharePoint, or OneDrive Pro, or requiring encryption between a user's Outlook client and the Office 365 datacenter to synchronize a user's mailbox content. The content is encrypted in transit, and the latest versions of Outlook that are required to access Office 365 (i.e.: Office 2007 SP2 or higher) encrypts content in the Offline Store file on the system.

Supporting International Regulatory Compliance

For organizations that have specific regulatory requirements for security that the organization needs to adhere to, Microsoft provides documented statements on their support for things like SAS-70, HIPAA / HITECH, 95/46/EC (aka: European Union Data Protection Directive), PCI Data Security standard, FISMA certification and accreditation, the Europe Union

Model Clause, and the like. A visit to the Microsoft Trust Center provides an organization information supporting Microsoft's compliance around these and other various regulatory compliance standards.

Addressing the Compliance Needs of Enterprises

What I've found over the years is that despite whatever Microsoft publishes as their support for security and compliance standards, the question still comes up, "is my data secure"? And with recent National Security Agency (NSA) leaks about access to information, organizations rightfully have a concern to what level their information is available to others.

For organizations that want to go beyond what is published and committed to by Microsoft for security, there are ways for an organization to own the "keys" for the encrypted content of their organization. Part of Office 365 is the option of leveraging Rights Management Services, or RMS. RMS is most commonly used for data leakage protection (DLP) where an organization can have key email messages and message attachments encrypted to prevent the content from being forwarded to someone else either inside the organization or externally. Only someone with an RMS key can open the content.

RMS keys are tied to a user's Active Directory account, thus the user (and ultimately the organization) owns the keys to the content that is encrypted with RMS. Even if Microsoft is subpoenaed to release information, the information released will be encrypted blobs of content. A second subpoena would have to be issued to the organization to release the keys to unencrypt the content. In this process, the organization will be directly made aware that information is being requested to be unencrypted, and can seek legal action to prevent the decryption of their content.

Setting an RMS Encryption Policy on Content

RMS encryption can be set on all email content (both in transit and at rest) as well as applied to content stored in SharePoint Online and OneDrive Pro stores. Policies can be automatically applied on the backend to intercept all messages in transit and at rest.

Built-in Single Sign-on and 3rd Party Authentication Mechanisms

It is common practice these days to tie user's logon and access to Office 365 to an organization's Active Directory, and Microsoft provides a couple methods to simplify the logon process for users, as well as supports 3rd party single sign-on tool integration. In all of these AD directory integration solutions, the goal is to ensure that if a user is terminated and their Active Directory account is disabled, that the user cannot access any information in Office 365. The AD integration prevents direct Web access to the content, and as such, Active Directory becomes the regulator of access to Office 365 information.

Microsoft provides integration using Active Directory Federation Services (ADFS) that links an organization's on premise Active Directory to Office 365. Some organizations may have other single sign-on solutions in their enterprise like Okta, Ping Identity, OneLogin, or the like. These 3rd party authentication products have connectors that tie into Office 365 for integrated authentication. ADFS and 3rd party integration into Office 365 is something that is a proven process and easily setup for directory integration.

Beyond ADFS or 3rd party directory integration, an organization would want content in their Active Directory one-way synchronized up to Office 365, information such as key Active Directory Groups (aka Distribution Lists) and user contacts. Microsoft provides a DirSync utility that can be installed on a server in the organization's environment that pushes content up from Active Directory to Office 365. That way as an AD Group is created, the group is displayed in Office 365.

Organizations can also use DirSync to perform a one-way transfer of a password hash that then eliminates the need for the organization to setup ADFS for authentication. The password hash is used by Office 365 to allow a user access to Office 365 content in the event that the organization's Active Directory is offline. With ADFS and other 3rd party single sign-on solutions, if Active Directory is offline, which could simply be a datacenter where Active Directory resides is disconnected from the Internet, users cannot authenticate to ADFS and thus cannot access Office 365 content. However by leveraging DirSync with the password hash, Active Directory can be temporarily offline, and users can still logon directly to Office 365. There are pros and cons of using ADFS or 3rd party authentication tools, or the DirSync password sync method that should be evaluated as part of the plan in migrating to Office 365.

Thoughts and Questions

- What is your current requirements for uptime of email? (99.9%?, 99.99%?, 99.999%?)
- What has historically been your total planned and unplanned uptime for email over the past 6 months? Over the past year? (this includes any downtime caused by patching, updating, and server reboots)
- Does Microsoft's regional datacenter failover capabilities meet your organization's expectation for high availability and redundancy?
- What regulatory compliance requirements does your organization have, and how do they match up with Microsoft's support for compliance?
- Would owning your keys for content stored in Office 365 address any additional security concerns you may have not already addressed by Microsoft's security practices?
- Do you have a single sign-on solution that you would like to integrate with Office 365, or will ADFS and/or DirSync provided by Microsoft meet your needs?

5 WHAT ABOUT ARCHIVING, RETENSION, AND E-DISCOVERY?

Typically in a conversation about security of email comes the topic of email archiving, email retention, and the ability to perform e-Discovery of content for regulatory or legal purposes. Email archiving, retention, and e-Discovery is part of the Office 365 offering.

Supporting Large User Mailbox Limits

With regard to email archiving and storage, Microsoft supports up to 50GB of mail per user in the user's personal mailbox. This used to be 10GB, was updated to 25GB, and most recently is 50GB storage limit. This is a LOT of email per user, many large enterprises have 5GB and 10GB limits, so by having the ability of up to 50GB, that is a lot of content to store. Many organizations may choose to set mailbox limits still to 10GB or 20GB despite Office 365 providing more storage. An organization can set whatever mailbox limit it wants up to the maximum limit offered by Microsoft.

Expanding Beyond Mailbox Limits with the Personal Archive

However, despite having such a large limit, there are always users who want or need more storage. Microsoft provides unlimited storage in personal archives within Office 365. Personal archives are like the old PST files that users have used for years, however instead of the PST residing on the user's workstation, the personal archive is stored in Office 365.

Additionally, when a user searches for messages in their mailbox (or the enterprise does an e-Discovery search for content) information stored in the personal archive also shows up in the search results just as if the content was in the user's primary mailbox.

Personal archives can have folders and sub-folders, so a user can organize content in their personal archives however they like. Mailbox rules can be setup by users to automatically move content from their mailbox to the user's personal archive. Microsoft currently provides no limit to the amount of data stored in a user's personal archive, as such, a user can store an unlimited amount of email (a very scary thought), but is fully supported by Office 365.

The only caveat to content stored in a user's personal archive is that content does not synchronize down to the user's offline store on their desktop or laptop system. Personal archive information is only in the cloud and the user has to be connected to Office 365 to search and access the content. So the most a user can "carry around" is 50GB of email, the rest of the mail is stored up in Office 365 for online search and access.

Built-in Retention Periods

So what happens when a user deletes a message, how do they recover the message? This is a multi-part answer as the deletion process of emails goes through stages. When a user deletes a message from their mailbox, the message will go into the user's "Deleted Items" folder. At any point, the user can go into their deleted items folder and move the message back into their inbox or move the message into any other folder. Some organizations set a 30-day period to have content in the Deleted Items folder to actually be deleted. This is not set by default by Microsoft in Office 365, so this is completely up to the organization to set a policy how long messages sit in the user's deleted items folder. Back when users were limited to 250mb of email or the organization wanted to minimize storage space for Exchange, the organization would set an aggressive 15 or 30 day deletion period of the Deleted Item folder content to just get rid of stuff. However when a user can now keep up to 50GB of email, information stored in the Deleted Items folder could be set to stay there nearly indefinitely. Again, this is up to the policy of the organization.

After content is deleted from the Deleted Item folder, either by an active organizational policy or if the user goes in and deletes the content manually out of the Deleted Item folder, the content will remain in Office 365 for a 15-day "retention period" (formerly called the Exchange dumpster). During this dumpster period, content can be undeleted by the Exchange/Office 365 administrator. After the dumpster period expires, the content is no longer accessible. Microsoft does not keep tapes of mailbox content and does not have the ability to go back months later to restore content. If the organization wants the ability to search and recover information beyond the dumpster retention period, see the section on "Utilizing Legal Hold on Mailboxes" a little later in this chapter.

Leveraging Retention Tags

For organizations that have regulatory requirements to retain content for a period of time, whether it is 3-yrs, or 7-yrs, or 25-yrs, content can be tagged with a retention tag either manually or automatically. Retention tags can be created in Outlook, and a message is tagged with the Retention Tag. Once tagged, content can be set by policy to not be deleted for the length of time denoted by the tag. Likewise, retention tags can be used to tag content that might automatically BE eliminated after a period of time, so content can automatically be deleted after say 10-days or after 30-days.

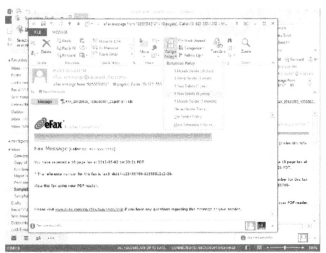

Setting a Retention Policy on a Message

An organization can setup retention tags and automatically have content that is sent, received, or stored go through content assessment and have a retention tag automatically applied to the content. This is configured by using transport rules (similar to user inbox rules, but instead configured in the Office 365 Exchange administration function by the administrator). Content can even be automatically encrypted using Rights Management Services encryption as part of the automatic identification, tagging, and encryption process.

Utilizing Legal Hold on Mailboxes

For organizations that have a legal requirement to retain content beyond what is provided in the default retention period or what can be done through retention tags, Microsoft provides a legal hold function for content in a user's mailbox AND personal archive. Legal hold is required by law for an individual who is under investigation and a notice is provided to the organization to protect evidence regarding a user or case.

Legal hold can be enabled by the Exchange/Office 365 administrator at any time simply by going into the Office 365 Exchange administration console, selecting compliance, choosing the user, and enabling Legal Hold status on the user's mailbox and archives. Content thereafter will be retained indefinitely until the user is taken off Legal Hold. Even if a user deletes content from their mailbox, and deletes the content from their Delete Items folder, while the messages do not show up in the user's mailbox and is not visible to the user, all content, all changes to the content, all records for content deletion are retained and is fully searchable, exportable, and reportable.

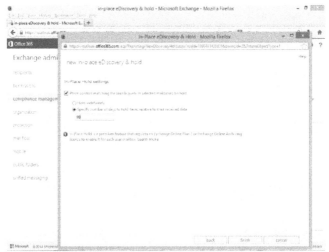

Setting a Mailbox on Legal Hold for Content Retention

Organizations that want to save all information for users and wants the ability to effectively undelete content beyond the default retention period could put all of its users on Legal Hold. This strategy can maintain the storage of content indefinitely, however legal counsel of many organizations will frown upon a blanket policy where data retention of information is maintained forever. An organization that has a policy of indefinite data retention opens up the door for legal inquiry and access to evidence far beyond what an organization may choose to want to be liable for. However in any case, an organization does have the ability of retaining content and accessing the content at any time.

Searching Content with Built-in e-Discovery

So with all of this data stored in Office 365, whether it is information stored in a user's mailbox or content that is stored in a user's personal archive, the key is to be able to retrieve the information in a case of e-Discovery. Office 365 provides built-in tools for e-Discovery. E-Discovery is an administration role that the Office 365 administrator can delegate the role to individuals. There are various e-Discovery roles, from someone who has the ability to kick off a search of content, to someone who has the ability of actually looking at and accessing the information. Many times a person in I.T. will be assigned the task to create a search and export content, however that individual may not have the right to view or access the content due to privacy concerns. As such, different roles for different purposes are available in Office 365.

Case Management in SharePoint to Support eDiscovery Queries

When content is searched, the search administrator can specify all of the common search criteria such as From whom, To whom, dates of search, keywords to search for, and information is then queried and identified. Office 365 maintains not only the current message, but also any variation to the message such as a version of the message that was received or sent, any modifications (edits) to the message that were saved, and copies of messages that were deleted. A search returns an exhaustive trail of a message which in itself is telling and commonly used as evidence if a user caught wind of an investigation and started to modify and delete certain messages, the eDiscovery agents can go in and specifically look at what information was being attempted to be deleted or altered.

A search identifies the number of messages that are found, which the search administrator can run different queries to garner different results. Once the correct search criteria is identified, the content can be set to be exported either into a mailbox with temporary access by a content reviewer, or exported to a PST file that could be burned to disc and distributed outside of the organization as requested in legal proceedings.

Office 365, in conjunction with a SharePoint Case Management function can extend email eDiscovery search to also include searching and putting on legal hold content that resides in SharePoint Online as well as Lync instant messaging conversations. The Case Management process in SharePoint provides more records management processing of information including assigning internal (and external) access to content in an online manner.

Transferring Existing Archives and eDiscovery Content to Office 365

For many organizations, they already have an existing email archiving and eDiscovery tool in place such as Symantec Enterprise Vault, Mimosa NearPoint, Zantaz, and the like. A common question is how to get that content up to Office 365.

Being that millions of mailboxes are being migrated to Office 365, an entire 3rd party ecosystem has emerged to handle the migration of archive content to Office 365. Tools from companies like TransVault, Archive360, and the like will extract content from existing archiving solutions and move the content into Office 365. Additionally, the various tools will also encrypt and encapsulate content that is in archives and potentially on legal hold as evidence to preserve the content in transit. That way the organization can certify that the content has been moved in a manner that retains the integrity of the content in transit.

And as content is then stored in an Office 365 account that has been put on legal hold, the preservation of integrity of the content is maintained in the Office 365 repository thereafter.

Thoughts and Questions

- Is 50GB of email enough for the bulk of your users?
- For users that have a need to retain more than 50GB of emails, will the use of Personal Archives meet the needs of the users?
- Does the organization have existing archived content that it needs to migrate to Office 365?
- How is legal hold handled today?
- Will content put on legal hold in Office 365 satisfy the organization's need to retain and protect content it is required to uphold?

6 HOW WELL ARE MOBILE DEVICES SUPPORTED?

Access by Windows systems as well as by Mac users has already been addressed in previous chapters of this book, in this chapter, we're addressing mobile devices. These days, as laptops are turning into tablets with optional keyboards, and mobile phones are getting 5" and 6" screens, there's a blurring line what is considered a mini-laptop versus a big phone, but in any case, Office 365 has full support not only for large systems, but also small systems through mobile endpoint device support.

Full Support for ActiveSync

The most common method of accessing email from mobile devices has been through the use of ActiveSync. ActiveSync is the method that Microsoft Exchange has synchronized iPhones, iPads, Android phones, Windows mobile phones, and the like for years. Microsoft has full support for ActiveSync, and any device that uses ActiveSync continues to be supported.

Support for Blackberry Devices

There was a time when Blackberry support was absolutely imperative for organizations, however as Blackberry's market share has dipped, and ActiveSync devices have grown in popularity, the need for Blackberry support has decreased. Nevertheless, Office 365 has full support to synchronize Blackberry devices with Office 365.

One Wide and Two Wide Outlook Web App Format

As was noted in the section "Outlook Web App Experience for Office 365 Users" in chapter 3, Microsoft has greatly enhanced the Outlook Web App (OWA) experience for users. OWA supports all modern browsers and the look and feel between browsers and various operating systems is the same. Specific to mobile devices, Microsoft has a 1-wide, 2-wide, and 3-wide viewing mode in Outlook Web App where different mobile devices will view the exact same OWA information, but just showing 1 or 2 columns of content including the message and preview than a full 3-column view of a larger system. OWA has become a universal access method to Office 365 content because of the common full feature view.

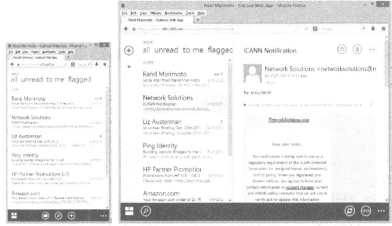

OWA 1-Wide for Phones OWA 2-Wide Format for Tablets

Mobile Device Policies and Management

Microsoft continues to provide mobile device polies and management over ActiveSync as it has done for years. In Office 365, the administrator can set a policy that users will be notified the first time they sync with Office 365 that they are subject to a specific company policy and to click to acknowledge they understand an enterprise policy has been implemented.

The enterprise policy could force the user to have a specific password policy length, how often they have to enter and re-enter their password on their mobile phone to access content, a policy can be set to push out a default Webpage that the user will get when accessing their browser.

An Office 365 administrator can set a single policy for the entire organization, or multiple policies that apply to different groups of users. All mobile phone policies are administered through the Office 365 Exchange administration section of the administrator's portal.

Wiping Mobile Devices

One policy that organizations commonly leverage is the Device Wipe policy. If a user loses their device, the administrator for the organization or the user themselves can enact a full device wipe. Typically the organization would encourage users to wipe their own devices the minute they suspect the device has been lost. Users do not have to embarrass themselves by asking someone else to wipe their device, but instead simply go into their Office 365 Outlook Web App mail screen, chose options, and under the phone option, to select their device and choose to send a wipe instruction to the device. If the user happens to find their device, they can simply resync their Office 365 mail, calendar, and contact information back down to the device. It would be presumed that if the user has personal data on the phone such as pictures, music files, and the like, that some form of device backup such as Apple's iCloud, has personal content that can be brought back down to the device after a wipe.

Users Can See their Mobile Sync'd Devices and
Choose to Wipe a Lost Device at any Time

Thoughts and Questions

- What type of devices does the organization support (iPads, iPhones, Android, etc)?
- Are the devices company owned subject to specific company policies, or personally owned by users with different policies for management available?
- Are there specific policies the organization applies to mobile devices such as password policies or support for device wipe?

HOW WELL ARE MOBILE DEVICES SUPPORTED?

7 DOES OFFICE 365 SUPPORT OUR MACS, IPADS, AND ANDROID DEVICES?

Access to Office 365 content for email, calendar, and contacts extends beyond Windows-based users these days to include Apple Macs, iPads, iPhones, and Android devices. While mobile devices were addressed in the previous chapter, and Outlook Web App was covered in Chapter 3, this chapter focuses specifically on non-Windows based endpoint devices.

Outlook for Macs

Apple Macs have entered the workforce and in many organizations make up 20%, 50%, or sometimes close to 100% of the user base. Thus having more than just adequate support for Macs to Office 365 becomes important for enterprises. Microsoft fully supports Office 2011 for Mac against Office 365, providing full access to emails, calendar appointments, contacts, and other messaging content. Rights Management System (RMS) encryption of content was addressed in Chapter 3, "How Secure and How Reliable is Office 365?" as a method to protect the leakage and security of content. Office 2011 for Mac fully support RMS, and as such, Macs users can also encrypt content and access RMS encrypted content for improved security.

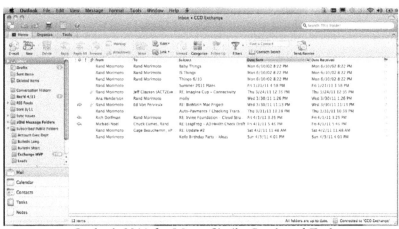

Outlook 2011 for Mac – Similar Look and Feel to
Outlook for Windows

The biggest complaint by Mac users against Office 365 is the inability to access Personal Archives from within the Office 2011 Mac client. Just like with the on premise version of Exchange 2013, to access Personal Archives, a Mac user has to drop into Outlook Web App (OWA) for access and search of the user's personal archives. Microsoft has committed to supporting archive access in the next release of Outlook for the Mac, however for now, OWA is needed by Mac users for archive content access.

Utilizing Microsoft's Remote Desktop Client

In the Fall of 2013, Microsoft released a series of Remote Desktop Client apps for Apple Macs, iOS, and Android that provides these endpoints access to a Windows-based Remote Desktop Service (formally known as a Terminal Service). These Remote Desktop Client apps are very eloquent versions that prior to Microsoft's release of these apps, users would have had to pay $10 or $20 for a comparable app.

The Remote Desktop Client apps from Microsoft support access through a RDS Gateway and load balancing facilitated by RDS Connection Brokers, so the latest in Remote Desktop Services access and security is supported in the apps.

Many Mac users who work in an office that has a Remote Desktop Service who want full access to Outlook and their personal archives use the Remote Desktop Client and access a Windows-based Outlook client. This new RDC client becomes yet another option for endpoint access.

Microsoft's Remote Desktop Client for Macs and iPads/iPhones

Outlook Web App for Mobile Devices

As covered in Chapter 6, the Outlook Web App access from a browser has been greatly enhanced with full support from all modern browsers from various endpoint operating systems. OWA has become a universal method of access email, calendar appointments, and contacts from various endpoints.

OWA App for Mobile Devices

In 2013, Microsoft released actual Outlook Apps for iOS and Android devices. The Outlook App is found by searching the respective online stores for OWA App. The OWA App adheres to Microsoft's common user interface and synchronization protocols, thus allowing a user of an endpoint device user the app to access their mail instead of the built-in app that might have come with their device, or a web browser access to their content. Search down the OWA App for mobile devices and see if it may provide better access to Office 365 content for mobile users.

Licensing that Supports Outlook for Windows and Macs Equally

Recent licensing changes by Microsoft now allows an organization to equally use a copy of Office for Windows users and Office for Mac users under the same license. In fact, Microsoft provides licensing that allows a user to install and access up to 5 copies of Office, so users can install a legal copy of Office on their work computer, work tablet device, home system, and personal mobile device all within the legal bounds of the license. Check the various options of Office 365 licensing to confirm that Microsoft Office use is included as part of the licensing you select to use.

Thoughts and Questions

- Are Apple Mac users expanding in terms of a percentage of users within your enterprise that you need to provide support for?

- Are iPads, iPhones, and Android devices common in your enterprise that you need to provide support access to mail, calendar, and contacts?
- Does your organization have a Remote Desktop Server (RDS) system in place that users can use the Remote Desktop Client apps that Microsoft has made available for various non-Windows based endpoint systems?
- Have you tried the OWA App that Microsoft has made available that is a native Outlook app for endpoint devices?

8 HOW DOES OFFICE 365 SUPPORT PUBLIC FOLDERS?

Several years ago Microsoft announced that they would get rid of Public Folders in Exchange, however over a decade since that statement, Public Folders are alive and kicking in Exchange 2013 as well as fully supported in Office 365. Granted, Public Folders has not evolved over the past decade and provide very basic functionality, however interestingly with Exchange 2013 and Office 365, Microsoft's public folders are not only supported, but actually do more today than they did years before.

Accessing Office 365 Public Folders for Office 365 Users

For organizations that can move their public folders to Office 365, the organization can include public folder migration as part of their migration to Office 365. Office 365 users have full access to Office 365 public folders. Microsoft made some changes to public folders with Exchange 2013 and Office 365. Instead of a monolithic public folder "database", Microsoft has converted each public folder into a mailbox, and the various mailboxes are linked together into a Public Folder hierarchy. So as far as users are concerned, their public folder hierarchy and access remain exactly the same as in the past, on the backend though, the public folders are actually mailboxes.

As mailboxes, each public folder is limited to 50GB of stored content, and an organization can have no more than 50 public folder containers, thus a maximum limit of 2.5TB of storage in public folders at the time of this book writing (February/2014). Public folder migration works great for organizations where these limits are acceptable in usage. For organizations that have extensive storage demands of public folders, or a lot of public folders, the organization either needs to do some housecleaning of public folders, or keep the public folders on premise.

Accessing On-Premise Public Folders for Office 365 Users

For organizations that have an extensive use of Public Folders and/or has extensive customization that triggers business processes, the organization may choose to keep public folders on premise, and just move users to Office 365. Microsoft fully supports this hybrid model for public folder access. All that is required is the Nov/2012 update to Office 2007, 2010, and 2013 that has the appropriate hooks to allow a user to access their email, calendar, and contact information up in Office 365, and connect to public folders that are on premise.

Migrating Public Folders to Office 365

The migration of public folder content to Office 365 is done through the public folder migration tool. The tool takes the existing public folder hierarchy, replicates the hierarchy up in Office 365, and the content in the public folders is moved to Office 365.

Public folder permission are migrated as part of the process as well. Because public folders in Office 365 are mailboxes, unlike older Public Folders in Exchange, public folders in Office 365 can have extensive inbox rules created for the folders. Many organizations have customized public folders to automatically do things through the user of scripts and agents. With mailbox rules, organizations now have the flexibility to do a lot more. As part of the migration process, organizations need to identify any customized rules or processes that were configured in their old public folders, and create equivalent mailbox rules to address similar functionality.

Additional Functions in Office 365 Public Folders

Other functions in Office 365 public folders beyond mailbox rules includes mailbox delegation as well as more extensive mailbox access permissions. In the past, an organization may have had a public folder moderator. In Office 365, the organization can actually set mailbox delegates who can manage and administer public folders just like a calendar or mail delegate does with user mailboxes. Between mailbox rules and mailbox delegates, an organization can automate tasks and set access rules needed for the organization.

Specific to access permissions, beyond just read/write access to the containers, permissions can be configured just like a mailbox. A container can be setup as a mailbox repository, calendar repository, or contacts repository. There are a number of variations that can be enabled for public folders.

Shifting from Public Folders to Other Shared Mediums

As much as Microsoft has committed to the continued support of public folders in Office 365, many organizations are taking this opportunity to eliminate public folders and user more dynamic methods of information sharing, collaboration, and access. One tool that has been around for a while is SharePoint. With SharePoint as part of Office 365, an organization can setup document libraries, rich content libraries, and store documents, video files, audio files, and the like in SharePoint. SharePoint content can be directly linked and made accessible both inside the organization and external to the organization, and from browser endpoints. SharePoint provides more access types and content storage types than public folders, and has been an option for many organizations moving away from public folders.

The new addition to Office 365, which is Yammer, is also an excellent solution for public folder replacement. Originally, public folders were used for common content so that instead of sending an email out to "All employees" that had a huge attachment on it, a user could simply post memos, messages, and large content in a public folder. So public folders were used as a replacement for "All employees" distributions.

Yammer provides a cloud-based solution for collaboration and communications for an enterprise. Within Yammer, a Yammer user can setup "groups" where each group can mirror a department, site, or workgroup within an enterprise. And Yammer Groups can also span beyond titles and roles, where Yammer Groups can be created for product groups, or even just general informational topic groups.

A memo can be posted to a Yammer group, multiple Yammer groups, or to the entire company. Users subscribe to the various groups, and as such can go look at the Yammer groups (similar to looking at public folders for new postings) and users can post content in the All Company area that is available to all employees of the organization.

So there are options for an organization to choose when looking to either migrate public folders, keep public folders on premise, or shift to a new tool like SharePoint and Yammer to get rid of public folders altogether.

Thoughts and Questions
- Are public folders still used in your enterprise?
- Are the public folders lightly used, or heavily used?

- Can public folder be migrated to Office 365 public folders, or will the organization choose an alternate route that might include keeping public folders on premise, or switching altogether to something new like SharePoint or Yammer?

9 WHAT ELSE IS IN OFFICE 365 FOR EMAIL USERS?

There were a handful of topics that either didn't fit in any of the previous chapters, or deserved additional content, as such, this chapter includes other things in Office 365 for mail users.

Tagging Content for Easy Search and Applying Policies

As mentioned in Chapter 5, Microsoft has the ability to tag messages, in Chapter 5 we were addressing tagging content for the purpose of identifying retention policies and rules. However content can also be tagged for things other than retention such as tagged to a project, tagged to a department, tagged as personal content, tagged as priority content, etc. Users can define their own tags and apply tags to content. Tags in Office 365 can also be color coded, so beyond just a label, a tag can be red, or green, or blue to more easily identify the content.

Once tagged, content can be more easily searched or policies can be applied to the searched content. As an example, content tagged to a specific project can be searched to find project related content instead of simply doing a global search for keywords that'll find anything and everything with the words in the message, not stuff tagged to a project. Content tagging helps users better organize information.

Leveraging Data Leakage Protection Using Rights Management Services (RMS)

Data Leakage Protection and Rights Management Services has been addressed a couple times already in this book as it relates to the automatic encryption of content for security purposes. A good business case of RMS encryption is in a world where users are working off of personal devices in a Bring Your Own Device (BYOD) environment. As much as Office 365 can allow a user or enterprise to wipe a device, many times users do not want their personal devices wiped. The personal device may include photos, audio files, and other content the user has not backed up. The personal device may also include email from other email systems the user connects to. So how does the organization protect content when it cannot protect and wipe the endpoint device? That's where RMS fits in.

An organization that encrypts all email messages, attachments, and document files that are keyed to RMS keys has little to worry about if the device is lost since the critical business content is RMS encrypted. Additionally, if a user takes an attachment and drops it into a Box.net, or Dropbox, or Google Docs folder and forgets the content is confidential information, the user may inadvertently be making protected information available outside of the enterprise. However if the content was RMS encrypted, even if the user accidentally (or purposely) saved content to a shared location, the content is encrypted, and unless someone has RMS rights to open the content, the content is inaccessible.

And furthermore, if the employee is terminated and their Active Directory account is disabled, even if the user has files, messages, content stored on their laptop, in a personal folder, even personally backed up to their personal iCloud backup, the content can only be accessed by someone with Active Directory credentials.

RMS extends far beyond content security and can assist an organization in addressing BYOD, cloud-storage, and other challenges where organization data gets outside of the organization.

Taking Advantage of Office 365 Apps

Office 365 supports what Microsoft calls Office 365 Apps. There are a handful of apps that come with Office 365 by default, and the organization can download and install other Apps into the Office 365 Administration Exchange console for the enterprise. Some of the default apps include a Bing Maps app that maps locations noted in emails or calendar appointments so that instead of cutting and pasting addresses into an external map application, a user can simply click on the top of the Outlook or OWA app to expose mapping information.

Bing Maps App Adds in a Map to an Email Message

Another app that is installed by default searches a message for words that typically would indicate a response is required or action is required. This app helps users focus on any action items needed out of a message. Other apps that are available include apps that connect a user to social media services like LinkedIn or Twitter, or other apps that extend data into cloud storage, client relationship management apps, and the like.

Thoughts and Questions

- Does your organization support BYOD for users where data is being stored on personal devices, and the management, protection, and control of the data could be better managed if the content was encrypted with RMS?

- Can content tagging help users more easily find information that they are looking for?

- Can users be trained on how Office 365 apps can simplify tasks they do today, and potentially other apps the organization can download and install that add even more value to users?

10 WHAT DOES AN EMAIL MIGRATION TO OFFICE 365 LOOK LIKE?

With a good background on what Office 365 includes for email functionality and administration, now to look at what the migration process to Office 365 looks like.

Confirming Pre-Requisites

Migrating to Office 365 has a handful of pre-requisites, both in terms of what is supported for the migration tool, but also the version of the Outlook client has to match up with what Microsoft requires for support. The pre-requisites have varied over time as Microsoft continues to roll in new features, functions, and thus new requirements for pre-requisites, so it is important to check at the time of your planned migration specifically what is required.

But at the time of the writing of this book (February/2014), the requirements for a co-existence migration of on premise Exchange to Office 365 is a requirement of Exchange 2007 Services Pack 3 or higher. This co-existence migration presumes effectively a "drag/drop" movement of content from the on premise Exchange to Office 365.

Microsoft does support just a straight mailbox export move from previous versions of Exchange as well as from non-Exchange based email systems.   So this co-existence migration maintains user's calendar appointments, and mailboxes are moved seamlessly in the background, even potentially in the middle of the day when the user is in their mailbox.

On the client end, Microsoft requires Outlook 2007 SP2 or higher for all Windows-based clients, and Office 2011 for the Mac for all Apple Mac-based clients.

For organizations that may be running Exchange in another hosted cloud provider environment where the Office 365 migration tools cannot be configured to access the Exchange databases directly, or the organization is migrating from something like Google Gmail or the like, there is a whole ecosystem of 3rd party migration tools from companies like MigrationWiz, Binary Tree, and the like that are available that extracts all messages, calendars, and contact information just as if the user were downloading their Outlook profile and message content to an offline cached copy. These tools can be purchased on a 1-time basis on a per user basis.

Establishing an Office 365 Tenant Account

Once the organization has a handle on the pre-requisites, an Office 365 Tenant account needs to be established. There are various ways to setup the Tenant account, whether the organization setups a 30-day trial first, then converts the trial to a paid for account. Or setup the account by having a credit card ready and buying a subscription where the monthly fees are charged to the credit card each month. Or for enterprise customers that have bought a Microsoft Office 365 subscription as part of their Enterprise License Agreement, there are onboarding mechanisms to activate license subscription rights to the Enterprise Agreement purchased. To setup a trial account or pay by credit card, go to http://office.microsoft.com/en-us/try/. If you have an Enterprise License Agreement, see your Microsoft representative or consulting partner for the proper onboarding process.

What you will be prompted for during the onboarding process is a handful of information that will establish your account including:

- Your name and a non-company email address: This would typically be a personal email address. It is used in case your Office 365 tenant is not available, the personal email address can be used for communications from Microsoft about your tenant account.
- Your company name and address: This is typical business information
- A tenant name for your subscription: Many times this could be similar to your company internet domain name (without the .com, .net, .org, .edu type suffix (i.e.: companyabc), however you may find the tenant name you choose is not available and you need to pick something else. The tenant name will appear in a handful of administrative task screens, and you'll identify your organization for support with Microsoft by this tenant

name. However once you integrate Office 365 with your enterprise Active Directory and attach your organization's true Internet domain, your users will never see this tenant name. For those who have run Exchange for years in the past, this is similar to the Exchange "Organization" name that for the most part was only ever visible by the administrator.

- <u>Your consulting partner company name:</u> Microsoft associates your tenant to a consulting partner you are working with. This is the partner that is typically assisting you with (or will be assist you with) the implementation and ongoing support of Office 365. When there is an Office 365 problem, not only will you be notified, but this consulting partner will be notified so that you have assistance available in your Office 365 implementation and ongoing support efforts.

Configuring DirSync, ADFS, DNS Settings, and Hybrid Coexistence

With your Office 365 tenant established, the next step is to integrate your existing Active Directory and Exchange environment into Office 365. If you don't have Active Directory, Microsoft provides a full directory including logon authentication to Office 365, so AD integration is NOT a requirement. However for organizations with Active Directory, the integration of AD to Office 365 minimizes users from having multiple logon names and passwords, and when the user's AD account is disabled, their access to Office 365 is disabled.

Likewise, an organization does not need to have a previous version of Exchange to run Office 365, Microsoft supports the migration of other email systems to Office 365. Where this section refers to a hybrid coexistence to Office 365 from Exchange, this presumes the organization has an existing Exchange 2007 SP3 or higher environment for co-existence.

For single sign-on authentication from an existing Active Directory to Office 365, the organization has 3 options, either using Active Directory Federation Service (ADFS) integration, use DirSync with password sync, or use a 3rd party directory authentication tool like Okta, Ping, or OneLogin. For organizations using ADFS or a 3rd party authentication tool, since access to Office 365 depends on real time validation back to Active Directory, it is important to have proper redundancy and resilience with the ADFS tool. DirSync with password sync sends a hash copy of the user password to Microsoft so that during the cache period of the sync, a user can still logon to Office 365 even though Active Directory is offline.

DirSync is setup to send Active Directory information to Office 365 such as distribution lists and mailbox contacts. This information keeps

Active Directory information on premise in sync with what users will see in the Office 365 directory.

There are DNS settings that need to be configured for mail routing, autodiscover, and Outlook Web App access among other configuration settings. This books won't go into the step by step configuration setup, so looking through the Microsoft Office 365 configuration guide as it is updated by Microsoft from time to time is important.

For organizations doing a Hybrid configuration, an existing Exchange server is maintain in the organizations datacenter that will remain online and available for administration, management, and potentially having user mailboxes retained on the hybrid server(s). The hybrid configuration allows organizations with mailboxes split between Office 365 and on premise to be able to share calendar free/busy information, access the organization's public folders that are on premise, and allow for mailboxes to be moved back and forth between on premise Exchange and Office 365.

Moving a Handful of Mailboxes to Office 365 to Test the Process

Once the Office 365 tenant is established and basic integration functionality is configured, the organization will typically migrate a couple mailboxes to Office 365 both to confirm the migration process works, and to begin documentation of any "quirks" the organization may want to be aware of that can either be fine-tuned and cleaned up, or users notified prior to the migration of their mailboxes.

Staging an Initial Move of Users to Office 365

After the basic migration tests confirm that everything is setup right, mail messages are flowing properly both in and out of both the on premise environment and the Office 365 environment, and the first couple mailboxes have migrated fine, then a larger group of users can be migrated.

This larger group is usually an initial half dozen mailboxes to re-validate that the migration process is the same as the initial couple mailboxes, and that everything is continuing to operate as planned. Once those users have been successfully migrated, another half-dozen or more mailboxes can be moved. This initial pilot phase will ensure clarity of what the migration of the full environment is expected to be when cutover.

Also during this initial move process, the amount of time it takes to move mailboxes can be calculated to determine how many mailboxes can be migrated at a time, and how long the mailboxes (both large and small) are taking to migrate.

Completing the Migration and Cutting Over Mailboxes

The cutover of balance of user mailboxes can be done all at once, or staged over several days or weekends based on how many users the organization has and how long it is taking to migrate mailboxes. Usually an organization can expect to move anywhere from 30-300 mailboxes in a night, and while a large bulk of users can be migrated at the same time, the organization needs to consider any help desk support considerations needed if users call in and need assistance.

The migration of mailboxes doesn't require someone sitting in front of a computer all night long and doing anything hands-on. The migration of mailboxes can be initiated through a PowerShell script and kicked off against a list of user mailboxes each night. Mailboxes that fail to migrate will report back as failed with a status. Mailboxes that migrate successfully will show up accordingly in the output of the migration script.

Even if a handful of mailboxes are still migrating as the new day begins, because Exchange 2007 SP3 or more current supports the migration of mailboxes in the background while users are in their mailbox, the migration of mail can proceed into the start of a work day without impact to the user.

Thoughts and Questions

- Based on the number of users and mailboxes you have, do you anticipate doing a single night cutover (assumed for organizations with fewer than 50-100 mailboxes) or stage the migration over several evenings or weekends?
- Do you have a Microsoft Enterprise License Agreement and have the Office 365 subscription activation information needed to tie your Office 365 tenant to the licenses you already have purchased?
- Have you reviewed the pre-requisites for Office 365 and have a plan to get any dependencies updated prior to connecting to Office 365 for the migration?
- Are you working with an Office 365 migration specialist that has done Office 365 migrations before that can provide guidance and assistance in your migration to Office 365?

11 EXTRA THINGS TO PLAN FOR THE MIGRATION

A migration to Office 365 is not something that is new or has an unknown process. Thousands of enterprises have already migrated to Office 365, and best practices have been developed in the migration process. It is important to note that Office 365 changes every 6 months or so with updates to the cloud service offering that also impacts the migration process. So it is important to have available current migration information as any quirks, issues, or processes that are over a year old are typically obsolete, and in most cases problems that have arisen in the past have been worked out and fixed by Microsoft after 6-12 months, and are not an issue anymore. However, there are a handful of things that do come up as part of the migration that at the time of this writing (February/2014) are noted in this chapter.

Migrating Delegates at the Same Time

When migrating users between an on premise instance of Exchange to Office 365, it is important for calendar delegates to be migrated at the same time. This is an Executive / Exec Admin relationship that exists where an Exec Admin manages the calendar of another individual as a calendar delegate.

While Office 365 provides a hybrid mode where free/busy calendar information is shared between users in Office 365 and Exchange on premise, the delegate needs to see more than just free/busy information and needs direct access and control to the Executive's calendar. As such, the Exec and the Exec Admin need to either both be in Exchange on premise, or both be in Office 365 at the same time. This will facilitate what is needed to share, manage, and administer calendars.

Preparing to Potentially Have to Resync Mail for Some Mobile Devices

After a mailbox is migrated to Office 365, the Office client for Windows and Macs will almost always just reconnect to Office 365 and work without a problem. The Outlook "profile" will repoint itself automatically to Office 365, and the user will not have to resynchronize their mail at all after the migration.

However, for some devices, most frequently Android phones, the endpoint mobile device has to completely resync the mobile phone email, calendar, and contact information. This resync is also needed on occasion for Windows Outlook users, Apple Mac Outlook users, and even Windows Phone and iOS users. This is something an organization can test during the pilot phase to migrate a handful of mailboxes where the users have a variety of endpoint mobile devices and endpoint versions of Outlook. This test will validate the anticipated experience of users being migrated and whether a resync of content is required.

Even after a mailbox has been migrated and the client seems to be working fine immediately afterward, but then on occasion messages get stuck and don't appear to be sending, or incoming messages don't appear to be arriving as expected, if it is convenient to rebuild a user's Outlook profile, or delete user's profile on a phone and configure the ActiveSync for the phone to connect the user all over again and bring down their data, that usually solves the problem faster than trying to debug specifically what is wrong with a specific device for a specific configuration.

Again, this is the value of the pilot phase, to not just test a handful of users that all have the same make, model, and configuration of systems, but to try to get a good sampling of systems that is indicative of the general make-up of the environment to test various migration scenarios.

Training Users on the New Outlook Web Access Interface

Another task that is helpful to prepare for is any training that might be needed after migrating to Office 365. Users will likely end up with a different Outlook Web App URL that they need to save to their favorites. Users may find the new Outlook Web App (OWA) to be a little different than what users are familiar with and might want some training on the new OWA interface. For the most part, the OWA client looks and operates just like Outlook has done so for years, so we don't find heavy training is required for all users.

Once again, an opportunity to use the pilot period to migrate over a handful of users, even novice users who the organization might identify as "usually needing support and guidance" and see whether the cutover to Office 365 is different enough that training or documented guidance is required.

Having Clear Expectations of Hybrid Coexistence

Office 365 provides hybrid coexistence so that an organization can have some users in Office 365 and some users remain on premise in Exchange. While this coexistence is the expected condition during a staged migration, and an organization may find it in a coexistence model for several weeks, other organizations look to make the hybrid mode their standard ongoing configuration for their enterprise.

The hybrid mode works fine if specific workgroups of users remain on premise and specific workgroups are migrated to Office 365, such as all Retail Sales associates in the field are moved to Office 365, but all corporate headquarter users remain on Office 365.

Challenges arise when users within a workgroup are split with some in Office 365 and some on premise. While Office 365 provides the ability to see free/busy calendar information for users that are split between Office 365 and on premise, as was noted earlier in this chapter, for calendar delegates, they need to be both in Office 365 --or-- both on premise, you do not want to split the delegates. But likewise in a department, a manager may be used to seeing calendar appointments of employees to book meetings, but if the department is split with some users in Office 365 and some on premise, that manager may not see the same information they expect.

If at all possible, an organization should consider migrating completely to Office 365 and get rid of the on premise instance, however we do know that some organizations like to have the hybrid model to "test out" Office 365 before they fully commit everyone to be migrated. In those cases, it's best to identify what criteria is needed before all users are migrated, so if it is to run Office 365 for 6 months without interruption incident or that the performance of Office 365 is the same as before, then the organization can check off any test requirements and then complete their full migration to Office 365 when their "must have" requirements have been met.

Planning for the Migration of Archives

As was covered in Chapter 5, "What About Archiving, Retention, and e-Discovery," organizations that have existing archive information in a 3rd party archiving solution will need to plan for the migration of content to

Office 365. Chapter 5 covers the options available for migrating content and managing archived data, so I won't cover it again in this chapter. Just noting that archive content needs to be addressed as part of the migration planning process, and then data can be moved to Office 365 as part of the plan.

Identifying 3rd Party Plug-ins for Replacement

As with any migration of Exchange, addressing any add-ins or plug-ins is important in the migration process. This might be things like Fax systems, List Manager tools, Client Relationship Manager integration tools, 3rd party voicemail systems, and the like. What organizations will find is many integrated applications are installed on the Outlook client end, and not on the Exchange server backend side. Things like CRM tools are typically Outlook client based. If the organization doesn't plan to change the version of Outlook as part of the migration to Office 365, then the CRM tool usually is not impacted even if the mail, contact, and calendar information is moved to Office 365.

Faxing software usually sits on a server in the organization's datacenter. Microsoft does not provide backend fax services in Office 365, however most fax software in the past 3-4 years have been updated to allow faxes to continue to come into an organization's datacenter, and the fax is then forwarded on to the Exchange server, in this case now, the fax content goes to Office 365.

Voicemail works the same way, where most voicemail systems have been updated so that instead of requiring an agent installed on the Exchange server, the voicemail server simply sends the voicemail as an attachment into Office 365. For voicemail, organizations can even consider using Microsoft's built-in Unified Messaging in Office 365 and have Office 365 be the voicemail system for the organization.

Usually there are solutions available with upgrades or updates to software that support Office 365. The good thing is the most common "add-ins" to Exchange have been anti-malware and backup software, which with Office 365, Microsoft takes care of those functions and the organization doesn't need to worry about Office 365 support for those functions.

Thoughts and Questions

- Do you have a list of 3rd party plug ins to Exchange and Outlook in use today that you need to work through the list to confirm successful operation in an Office 365 environment?
- Do you have a list of Admin / Exec Admins that do calendar delegation to ensure those groups of users are migrated together

during the process?

- Do you have a list of users in a working group that should be maintained together during the migration process?
- Do you have a 3rd party archiving solution that needs to be addressed in the migration of email archives to Office 365?

EXTRA THINGS TO PLAN FOR THE MIGRATION?

12 WHAT'S LYNC LIKE IN OFFICE 365?

For those using Lync 2013 on premise, Lync in Office 365 is the same services for Instant Messaging, Presence, Web Conferencing, Lync to Lync Video, and Lync to Lync Voice. Because there's no "mailbox" of content that has to be migrated over, a Lync migration tends to be a quick cutover and users frequently never know they were moved to Lync in the cloud.

Everything but Voice Telephony

Microsoft's offering for Lync Online in Office 365 is effectively everything that Lync 2013 has on premise, however Microsoft currently does not provide telephony into the phone company. So you can do instant messaging internal and external to your organization. Lync Online provides Lync to Lync voice and video conferencing so that users with Lync clients can carry on voice and video sessions over the network and internet. Lync allows users to setup Web Conferences and share desktops, do group meetings, and as long as everyone has a headset or speaker / speakerphone for their system, they can participate in the Web meeting with full video, audio, and content sharing.

Microsoft Lync Client to Office 365

But if someone is driving in their car and wants to call into a toll free phone# to join a call, or if someone wants to call out of Office 365 to a business that has a regular phone or mobile phone number, Lync in Office 365 by default does not communicate with conventional phone systems.

Handling Telephony with Lync Online

So if Lync Online does everything that Lync 2013 does but traditional phone telephony, what does an organization do for phone services? There are a few options for telephony in Lync Online that includes integrating an existing non-Lync telephony system (like Cisco, Avaya, or the like) with Lync Online. Another option is to utilize one of Microsoft's telephony providers like InterCall that provides integrated telephony services with Lync Online. An organization that might already be using Lync 2013 on premise with telephony may choose to continue to keep Lync on premise (yet use everything else in Office 365 like email, SharePoint, and Yammer in the cloud). Or an organization can use a 3rd party hosted provider like a CallTower that provides hosted Lync 2013 with telephony for an organization.

For an organization that might already have a telephony on premise solution from someone like a Cisco, Avaya, or the like, the organization can continue to use the telephony of the existing on premise phone system, and then use Lync for everything else. The on premise phone service can be used for inbound and outbound calls, and the on premise phone system can be setup to forward voicemails into Office 365's Unified Messaging function so that even voicemails are part of Office 365.

The option where an organization can use Office 365 for Lync and sign-up with someone like InterCall will allow the organization to have inbound and outbound phone calls and call-in numbers for Lync Web Conferences hosted by one of these Microsoft integrated telephony providers. These providers have competitive telephony costs for phone calls paid for no a flat rate basis or on a per minute basis.

For organizations that already have Lync 2013 setup and potentially even using Lync for telephony, there's nothing wrong with using Office 365 for everything else, and just have Lync remain on premise. Office 365 providers integrated support so that the various products can be run standalone, integrated together, or integrated with other on premise services. Rumor has it that Microsoft will provide Lync Voice at some point in the future, and at that time, the organization can shift from Lync 2013 on premise to Lync Voice in Office 365 when it is available.

And lastly, the option with a 3rd party host cloud provider like a CallTower, there are service providers that have been hosting Lync and other telephony services in a cloud for some time now. If an organization wants to get rid of everyone on premise, or potentially has no telephony on premise that it wants to keep and wants to move to the cloud, connecting up with a CallTower for Lync and telephony can provide an organization a full voice solution. Lync hosters like CallTower can leverage existing Lync licensing that an organization may have, and they provide flat per user costs for a full Lync 2013 in the cloud service that includes all that Office 365 provides for Lync (instant messaging, Web Conferencing, Video/Audio Lync to Lync Conferencing) plus telephony. Various rate plans include unlimited domestic minutes and unlimited inbound calls, something that definitely makes the solution attractive for organizations with fewer than 200-300 users.

Getting Identical (or Better) Experience for Those Who Had Lync 2013 On-Premise

Lync in Office 365 provides the same Instant Messaging, Web Conferencing, Video/Audio Lync to Lync Conferencing capabilities, but without having to setup and manage servers on premise. For organizations that are currently paying extra for 3rd party Web Conferencing services like WebEx or GoToMeeting, the organization will likely find that Lync not only replaces the other Web Conferencing service, but provides full Web Conferencing plus all of the other Lync functionality at a flat cost per user per month.

Addressing Performance Queries about Lync in Office 365

A question that is commonly asked about a hosted version of Lync versus Lync on premise is whether the performance is acceptable. For performance, Web Conferencing tends to be the thing that a lot of users may be connected to sharing desktops, videos, and collaborating together. As organizations think about who they invite to these Web Conferences, they are typically Web Conferences that includes a handful of external users, and maybe just a couple internal users.

When an organization hosts their own Lync and their own Web Conferences, ALL communications both internal and external go through the organization's on premise Lync server(s). When Lync is run in Office 365, all users, internal and external, connect to Microsoft's Office 365 datacenters for Lync connectivity. If only a couple users in-house are connected to the Office 365 Lync meeting, then only a couple sessions are connected to the on premise network. All other users connect directly over the Internet to the Office 365 Lync environment. This tends to actually decrease the traffic on the network for an organization. And for organizations that are currently using externally hosted Web services, the bandwidth and communication demands would be similar from users connected to a WebEx session to the same users connected to an Office 365 Lync Web Conference session. So performance and bandwidth demands are not greatly different than what an organization has today.

Supporting Various EndPoint Devices

One of the big things with the latest version of Lync 2013 (and Lync in Office 365) is Microsoft's support for non-Windows based endpoints. For the longest time, Microsoft had great support for Windows systems, but terrible support for anything else. Over the past several months, Microsoft has released update after update for Lync endpoint clients that support Apple Macs, iPads, iPhones, Android devices, as well as a fully functional Web client.

Now on a Mac, a user can interact on Instant Messaging, Web Conferencing, Lync to Lync Video and Voice Conferencing with the same functionality as Windows users. The Mac user can start a Web meeting, join a Web meeting, share content, take control of another system, etc. This has been key to ensuring that Lync in Office 365 gains adoption when everyone in the enterprise (both Windows and Mac users) have equal functionality.

And having a full featured Web client has been critical as well. A few years back, when someone was invited to a Microsoft Web meeting, they had to actually install a full Lync 32-bit or 64-bit executable to join the meeting which pretty much was a deal killer in the enterprise when trying to invite external participants. Now, all a user needs is a browser and a browser-based Web client is enabled for Lync interaction. If an external participant doesn't have the Lync client installed, they can just choose to run the meeting in their Web browser, and they can fully participate in the conference.

Integrating Lync with Room Size Video Conferencing Systems

Microsoft has begun support room size video conferencing systems, not just connecting and supporting systems from Polycom or LifeSize, but full Microsoft Lync integrated systems. Microsoft has a solution called the Microsoft Lync Room System that includes large 50+ inch touch screen displays and wide angle cameras for full room integration. Microsoft has also partnered with companies like Smart Technologies that has traditionally been known for their digital write-on boards in classroom settings that dumps written content off the digital whiteboard to print or to an attachment. Smart Technologies integrates the white board plus a large screen video display and wide angle camera to create a full video, audio, whiteboard, desktop sharing solution.

Organizations acquiring these Microsoft integrated room size video systems have found it convenient to simply snap the room system into Lync for meeting scheduling, joining users, inviting users, and having full integration as just another Lync client endpoint.

Centralizing Logging and Conversation History

In this world of regulatory compliance and privacy protection, Lync provides centralized logging as well as tracked conversation history so that Instant Messaging conversations can automatically be saved and be discoverable in an e-Discovery search as required by law. Also the scheduling of Web meetings, audio calls, and video calls are tracked and logged, not that the audio nor video stream are captured by default, but more so just logging "that" a meeting or conversation took place.

Lync in Office 365 does support the capture of Web meetings so that the shared session display and the audio stream are captured and saved to file. This capturing of content is not particularly for regulatory purposes unless the meeting may need to be captured as a component of public records compliance, but more so for users who were unable to attend a meeting or access by attendees who wanted to go back to check on information presented.

Thoughts and Questions

- Does your organization currently have users that do Instant Messaging where you would like to centralize IM conversations and track them just like email messages to address regulatory compliance requirements?
- Does your organization use a variety of Web Conferencing services where a shift to Office 365's Lync Web meetings can potentially

save the organization a significant amount of money by consolidating Web meetings into Lync?

- For traditional phone telephony, do you plan to continue with your existing phone setup, or potentially integrate with one of the various solutions available based on Lync 2013 for your enterprise?
- Do you have a mix of endpoints (Macs, Windows, iPads, Android, etc) where having support for a wide range of clients be of help for the organization?

13 WHAT'S A MIGRATION OF LYNC TO OFFICE 365 LIKE?

For an organization looking to leverage Lync in Office 365, the switchover is more like a cutover than a migration. The organization needs to keep all of the users on the same system to maintain clean integration, and there are limited burdens which keeps the cutover relatively methodical.

Migrating Without the Burden of Data

Unlike email systems burdened with years of email and calendar appointments that need to be migrated, Lync for the most part doesn't have stored data that has to be transferred. This in itself greatly simplifies the cutover to Lync in Office 365. For most participants that have been running Lync on premise, a switchover of DNS settings to point users to Lync in Office 365 instead of Lync on premise resets the users Lync client to point to Office 365.

Needing to Resend Meeting Appointments

What does need to occur is a resending of meeting appointments that were sent originally with the on premise Lync, but now need to be resent with the Office 365 Lync meeting information. A quick search of a calendar for the meetings that users have organized, and an update of the Lync meeting information with an appointment "update," and the Web conference information gets updated with the new Office 365 Lync meeting information for participants.

If a user is just a participant in a meeting (not the originator), then the user doesn't have to resend anything. A participant of a Lync meeting, whether a participant from Lync on premise or a participant from Lync in Office 365 just joins meetings. So it's really only the person who is the meeting leader that has to resend meeting information.

Running Non-Lync Migrations in Parallel to Lync Online Operations

For organizations that may be using a non-Lync Web Conferencing system such as WebEx meetings or GoToMeetings can still be used for a short period of time. In fact, the organization can fully cut over to Lync in Office 365, new meetings can be sent out using the Lync Online, and old meetings can be run on WebEx or the like for a week or two until the user just replaces the meeting "Join Now information" with Lync Online info instead of WebEx or GoToMeeting information. This allows for a short time parallel operations until the users can transition fully to Lync in Office 365.

Choosing to Replace Handsets with Headsets

As users shift to using Lync Online's Voice over IP (VoIP) capabilities for audio communications instead of using mobile phones or a 3rd party dial-in service, the user's will likely want to shift away from a traditional desktop phone to a headset connected to their system. Traditional handsets are typically associated to a desk or office and is not portable for the users, so when the user moves their laptop or tablet from one office to another, or takes their mobile device on a business trip or home, they need a mobile headset to follow them.

There are plenty of headsets available, whether USB connected devices, Bluetooth devices, and wireless devices. Some new Bluetooth headsets that users use with their mobile phone can be dual-paired and connected not only to the mobile phone but also to a user's Bluetooth connection on their laptop or tablet system.

Headsets can travel with the user, so whether they take a call at the office, at a coffee shop, from a hotel room, or from home, they have connectivity to Lync communications.

Keeping Existing Handsets if Desired

Organizations that may be switching over from a telephony system like a Cisco CallManager system to one of the various 3rd party Lync Voice solutions may find they have a number of handsets that users want to keep and not want to switch to USB or Bluetooth headsets. In those cases, the organization has a couple choices. Either buy a new desktop handset for the user to work with Lync, or there are companies like NET that makes network switches that will accept Cisco phones and allow those phones to continue to work in Lync.

There are a variety of options available when working with desktop handsets, headsets, conference room phones, and other devices for telephony to streamline the cutover to Lync 2013 on premise, Lync in Office 365, or Lync in a 3rd party hosted voice service provider.

Thoughts and Questions

- If you are using a non-Lync Web Conferencing service, will you run Lync in Office 365 in parallel to the Web Conferencing service for a short period of time, or just have users cutover at some given date?
- If you are using Lync on premise and will be switching over to Lync in Office 365, can you have users who have sent meeting appointments identify their appointments with a search of their calendar and resend Lync meeting information to attendees?
- Will you be replacing desktop handsets with headsets as part of the transition to Lync in Office 365?
- Do you need to provide a transition from desktop handsets of non-Lync systems to a solution that works with Lync?

WHAT'S A MIGRATION OF LYNC TO OFFICE 365 LIKE?

14 GETTING THE MOST OUT OF SHAREPOINT ONLINE

SharePoint in earlier versions of Microsoft's Business Productivity Online Services (BPOS) and initial releases of Office 365 was not highly adopted by organizations because of the lack of features, customization, and options for SharePoint workspaces. However with the more recently updates to Office 365's SharePoint Online services that is built on SharePoint 2013, organizations are using SharePoint Online more and more.

Gaining Feature Parity with SharePoint On-Premise

The key to getting organizations to use SharePoint in Office 365 had to start with feature parity between SharePoint 2013 on premise and SharePoint in Office 365. SharePoint Online now provides similar templates for creating Team Sites, Media Stores, Business Workflow Sites, and the like that are similarly found in SharePoint 2013 on premise. Users can now do more than just post content and do version controlling, but actually add in Web Parts, create search criteria templates, build their own templates that users can choose from, integrate Yammer into SharePoint, and leverage the capabilities typically found in SharePoint 2013 into the SharePoint Online in Office 365.

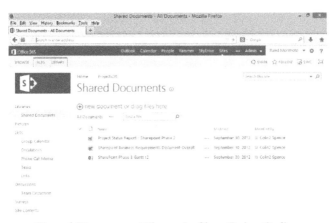

Shared Document Library in SharePoint Online

Getting Better Customization Options in SharePoint Online

Beyond just having similar features and functions in Office 365 that is found in SharePoint 2013 on premise, organizations can also customize SharePoint Online with custom skins, graphics, and settings. As Microsoft provides more customization options in SharePoint 2013 that is based on components in SharePoint rather than hardcoding the SharePoint or Web instances directly, the customization is more portable and can be applied to SharePoint in Office 365.

Remaining On-Premise for Highly Customized SharePoint Environments

While SharePoint Online has greatly improved the flexibility and customization options that has enabled it to gain adoption by enterprises, organizations can still choose to use SharePoint on premise. Unlike things like Exchange or Lync that require a formal hybrid integration to function, SharePoint can easily be split where some SharePoint sites are in Office 365, and some SharePoint sites are on premise or in other datacenters.

SharePoint is known only by the DNS name and pointers that redirect users between sites, so a hybrid integration, even cross integration between SharePoint 2007 or 2010 on premise can co-exist with SharePoint in Office 365. This provides organizations the flexibility to initially keep some existing SharePoint sites on premise that it has today, and build new functionality in Office 365 for new sites ongoing. Users are seamlessly redirected to Office 365 sites, and over time, an organization can shift more and more content up to Office 365.

Building Similar Templates Between On-Premise and SharePoint Online

For organizations that are using SharePoint 2013 on premise, similar templates can be created in Office 365 as well as in SharePoint 2013 on premise, thus keeping the look and feel the same, only having the destination of the content different and for the most part hidden from users.

Some of the common uses of this common template configuration is used by organizations that have distinctive internal content that has to be protected on premise like human resource information or potentially highly sensitive product development information that the organization chooses to keep on premise. However the organization may want to have externally facing sites where users outside of the organization can access and share other content. By having similar look, feel, and configuration of site templates, but a clear control between content that is on premise and content that is in Office 365, the organization allows for better secured control.

Leveraging Rights Management Services for Encrypted Content

In Chapter 9, "What Else is in Office 365 for Mail Users?" we covered Microsoft's Rights Management Services (RMS) for the encryption of email content that is tagged to user credentials in Active Directory. RMS can also be integrated into SharePoint Online. Content can be RMS encrypted and saved into SharePoint libraries, or an entire library can be configured with Information Rights Management settings so that any document stored in a document library takes on the RMS template encryption that has been defined.

An organization can configure a finance department document library such that any content saved in the document library can only be opened by someone in the Finance group. Or content that is saved in the ProductX site can only be accessed by members of the ProductX team. This RMS encryption follows the content no matter where it goes after it leaves the SharePoint library.

This means that if a user pulls a file out of the library, attaches it to an email or posts the file in a public file sharing system, the only users that can open the file are those that the document library policy stipulated. This is a great data leakage protection solution as an organization can tightly control access to content by policy.

Power BI for Office 365

Microsoft extends the power of business intelligence tools to Office 365 through its Power BI functionality. Power BI adds additional functionality in SharePoint. Power BI has connectors that connects SharePoint to external data sources, whether that's Excel spreadsheets, Microsoft SQL, Oracle, IBM DB2, MySQL, Sybase, PostgreSQL, Hadoop, Dynamics CRM, Microsoft Exchange, Facebook, oData feeds, Azure, and others.

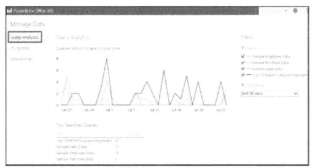

Managing Data with Power BI within Office 365

Power BI provides the ability for organizations to model and analyze data, virtualize information, share content, collaborate and data models, and create information insights on data sources. The information stored in Power BI can be accessible virtually anywhere from any device that connects to Office 365.

Microsoft also provides a number of extensions to Microsoft Excel with built-in components like PowerPivot as well as there are downloadable components like Power Query and Power Map. Data can be imported into Excel, tables can be linked, models can be developed, and ultimately charts can be generated to visually analyze the data.

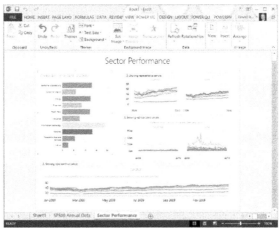

Using Power View to Display the Results of Data Analysis

Thoughts and Questions

- Are the features and functions included in Office 365 for SharePoint useful for future Sites that your organization may build up?
- Are there cases where you want to share content externally to your organization, and the facilities built in to Office 365 of supporting external users can be of benefit?
- Do you have an existing SharePoint on premise environment that you may migrate content in to SharePoint Online?
- Will a hybrid model with some SharePoint sites on premise and some SharePoint sites in Office 365 be a good short term or long term solution for your organization?
- Can the Power BI tools help your organization bring business intelligence, data analysis, and data modeling to users for faster and easier access to information?

15 LEVERAGING ONEDRIVE FOR CLOUD-BASED SHARED STORAGE

For organizations that are using cloud-based file sharing solutions like Box.net, Dropbox, or the like, OneDrive Pro that is built in to Office 365 can provide an organization similar file sharing capabilities, but something that is integrated into the license and the security model that Office 365 is built under.

Differentiating OneDrive versus OneDrive Pro

First of all, Microsoft has a couple products called OneDrive and it's important to differentiate between the two as they are different solutions. OneDrive is a public file storage solution that Microsoft provides via their Live.com service. OneDrive allows individuals to sign-up for a Live.com account and get anywhere from 7GB to 25GB of free storage space.

OneDrive Pro is the file storage solution that is built in to Office 365. OneDrive Pro is actually built on SharePoint 2013, so for users that are familiar with what Microsoft used to call "MySites" in SharePoint, OneDrive Pro is more like MySites than the commercially available OneDrive solution.

Each user in Office 365 gets a OneDrive Pro storage space where the user can store personal files as well as share files with others. The storage is in the cloud, and as such, a user can store information in OneDrive Pro and have the content available from any of their systems by simply reaching out to the Internet and pulling down content.

OneDrive Pro Document Library Space

Synchronizing OneDrive Pro Content to Systems

OneDrive Pro also has Apps that are available where content in OneDrive Pro can be synchronized down to endpoint devices so that a user can have information readily available on their laptop, tablet, or mobile device. With content synchronized down to an endpoint device, a user does not have to be connected to the Internet to access information. The information is available locally on their device.

Apps can be installed on multiple systems so that a user can have their content readily available from any of a number of systems that the user works from, and the information can be kept up to date across devices. Users no longer have to work from just a single device, copy content down to a thumb drive to have access to the content on various systems, nor do the users have to use third party cloud-based file storage solutions.

Replacing My Documents with OneDrive Pro

Also with the synchronized content, users can save information locally to their system and have that information store synchronized back up to Office 365. This provides users a backup mechanism to their content stores. Users who have used the My Documents feature in Windows will know that while the information is stored in the their My Documents folder, most of the time the content is not replicated or backed up in any manner, and thus the content only resides on a single system.

By having the ability to save content locally to the user's local OneDrive Pro location, the content is not only on the local system, but when the user connects to the Internet, the content can be automatically synchronized and uploaded up to Office 365 as a live backup of information.

OneDrive Pro is not limited to just Word docs and Excel spreadsheets, but effectively anything a user can save to a SharePoint Library, the user can save to OneDrive Pro. This includes non-Microsoft document files like Acrobat PDF files, MP3 audio files, WMV video files, CAD files, ISO image files, and the like.

Setting Policies with OneDrive Pro

OneDrive Pro, being a subset of SharePoint, allows organizations to set policies on the OneDrive Pro repository. Unlike other cloud service providers where content is frequently out of the reach of I.T. for security purposes, OneDrive Pro, being part of Office 365, at a minimum is protected by the Office 365 user logon credentials. If the user's Active Directory account is disabled, the user will no longer have access to the Office 365 OneDrive Pro content.

In addition to simple logon access to content, an Administrator in SharePoint Online can add themselves as the Site Administrator to user's OneDrive Pro (aka MySite collection). A Site Administrator can then apply permissions and policy changes to the OneDrive Pro collection, allowing (or blocking) users from synchronizing their content or sharing their content with others.

Synchronizing other SharePoint Libraries with the OneDrive Pro Client

The OneDrive Pro client provides the ability for a user to not only synchronize content that is in the user's personal OneDrive Pro folders, but also allows other libraries and media content in SharePoint Libraries in Office 365 to be selected and synchronized as well. This enables a user the flexibility to have access to personal as well as shared content while they are offline or mobile.

SharePoint library content is subject to check-in and check-out policies, and an administrator can set a SharePoint library to be blocked from being synchronized by users. Content protection and policy based access helps an organization maintain control of the content in libraries throughout the enterprise.

Encrypting Content in OneDrive Pro

As has been addressed a couple times now about the use of Microsoft's Rights Management Service (RMS) encryption both in Exchange (Chapter 4) and SharePoint (Chapter 14), content stored in OneDrive Pro can also be RMS encrypted. This can be a good strategy for users who want to protect and control data, that while they may open up a OneDrive Pro folder for shared access, the user may want to encrypt the content stored in that folder so that the recipient of the content does not inadvertently make the content available to others.

RMS protection can be placed on content for the OneDrive Pro owner and the individual they want to share the content with, but no others can be added with permissions.

Thoughts and Questions

- Do users in your organization use cloud-based file sharing solutions like Box.net or Dropbox today that the organization has limited or no control over the cloud hosted content?
- Does the organization want to have better control and better security of content where something like OneDrive Pro can provide shared file access, as well as tie access to user's credentials managed by the enterprise?
- Do users work from different devices and having the ability of mobile file access be an attractive option for users?
- Can encrypting content using Rights Management Services (RMS) add further levels of security on content protection, helping an organization better protect the intellectual property of the organization?

16 LEVERAGING YAMMER IN THE ENTERPRISE

Yammer is a new addition to the Microsoft Office 365 service offering. Microsoft acquired Yammer and has since included it as part of the Office 365 licensing for enterprises. Yammer is used as a centralized communications and collaboration tool, allowing users within an organization and outside of an organization to post messages, invoke feedback, and share content and ideas.

Enterprise Social Networks as a Feedback Mechanism

What many organizations lack is real-time feedback on whether or not what the company provides is helpful to its users. As much as a business analyst learns about the business they are analyzing, how its employees do their jobs and how the customers of the organization interact with the business, the key is to make sure the systems and processes that are put in place actually help employees become more effective at what they do, ultimately creating a benefit for the organization.

The feedback mechanism that many in Corporate I.T. don't understand quite yet, is "Social Media". When posed with the question whether an organization has an Enterprise Social Network and is leveraging social media, most in I.T. not only say they do not have a social media strategy in place, but they don't understand how it can help the business.

When we talk about social media, everyone likens it to Facebook, for the business and Twitter, for the enterprise. This doesn't help the organization relate Facebook or Twitter to being good for communications inside of a business. Back to the feedback mechanism, when a picture of say, the Golden Gate Bridge, is posted on Facebook, friends of that poster immediately knows where the person was and what they were doing. When an individual posts a political commentary on their Facebook page and their friends share their like or dislike of the topic, the person gets immediate feedback on how those associated with the person, feel about what has been shared.

Take this feedback mechanism into the enterprise, like implementing something like Yammer in the organization. The marketing department can post a picture of an upcoming marketing campaign and look to get feedback from employees on what they think. Employees can critique the planned campaign, get input on whether pictures from the planned ads might be too risqué, or controversial, or inappropriate, all through the internal social enterprise network feedback mechanism. The organization knows darn well that once the ad campaign hits the public, that the public social media engines, like Twitter and Instagram, will be filled with good and bad feedback. So rather than going straight to market, the organization can leverage feedback from its internal employee base first.

Similarly, instead of waiting until the last minute to share company strategy information with employees, the management team of an organization can have executives socialize strategy ideas with employees via the organization's social network system. If anything, the executives are giving employees an initial "heads up" that something is about to happen. Employees will be better looped in, and can more quickly ask questions and gain feedback on things, effectively giving the employee more of a say on what's going on, or at least hear directly from the executives of the organization and potentially have a Q&A to address queries in real time.

Transparency in Communications Leads to Clarity

Real time communications, the ability for employees to get information and receive responses back immediately improves the transparency in communications throughout the enterprise. The simple transparency of communications and employees feeling "looped in" to what's going on leads to higher employee satisfaction with the employee feeling like their management is listening to them and keeping them connected to the organization. The decision making of the organization will also improve by having employees provide input and immediate feedback to what's going on within their organizations.

The enterprise social networks and tools like them that users have been using in their personal interactions for a while now, and potentially may even be using for business purposes via external cloud resources, are important for I.T. to understand, both in terms of existence as well as use cases. It's important for I.T. to determine how they can provide similar services or simply get their arms around the tools in use, to maintain data privacy and confidentiality, or any other responsibilities of the organization.

Empowerment and Engagement

The typical organizational structure found in most companies is an obstacle to collaboration, especially across business units. Typical cross-department collaboration groups are laboriously established over existing reporting relationships and to address carefully planned needs. Tapping the benefits of informal relationships and natural collaboration requires a new approach and new tools.

In addition to the top down structuring of collaboration efforts, there are enormous benefits to allow users throughout the organization the ability to develop complex networks and relationships that do not follow the organizational structure and then leverage those connections for collaboration. Giving users the ability to select their own collaborative groups and participate in efforts that they can improve will result in better engagement across the organization, increased job satisfaction and improved employee efficiency and effectiveness.

While engagement and empowerment will not be leveraged by all users equally, the advantages and momentum created by those who adopt the approach quickly and fully will serve to improve the overall engagement and performance of other users and even positively impact those users that are last to engage. The metrics provided around engagement and leadership within the collaboration system can then be used to identify those individuals who go above and beyond for the organization, have valuable insights within and outside their role could make good candidates for investment and advancement.

Collaborating with Yammer

Yammer is first and foremost a chat platform. It is a sophisticated and manageable platform to hold written conversations with a flexible audience. The overall interface and feature set of the platform is designed to facilitate conversations between participants both internal and external to the organization. The information in the conversation can include several formats and media types and can be consumed using a variety of clients on most common platforms.

The large volume of conversations that occur in a typical organization would quickly become unmanageable for users and IT alike. To address this issue, conversations in Yammer are organized around groups. Groups can be created by authorized users and while by default they are open to promote collaboration and transparency, they can be protected in the event that they are expected to handle confidential or sensitive information.

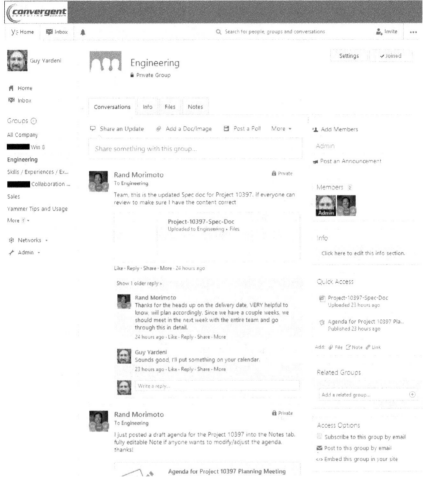

Communicating within Yammer to share content and ideas with feedback

Of course, collaboration would be of limited value if it was restricted to users internal to the organization. The security and confidentiality issues that are inherent in collaboration with external entities are addressed in Yammer by the creation of External Networks. External Networks support members that are outside the organization and support the creation of multiple groups within each network.

Chat based conversations are in themselves a very powerful collaboration tool. However, Yammer extends the power of the collaboration platform by including several additional collaboration tools to augment and enhance the conversations. Each group or network has a file repository associated with it. These files can be linked into conversation, edited online – using Office Web Apps if they are Office documents, support version tracking and provide automatic change notifications. In addition to the files, each group and network includes the capability to create notes, a powerful collaborative feature that supports simultaneous edits by multiple members along with identification of which member made each change. Web links can also be added to each group to provide quick access to related information, whether it is within Yammer or not. Finally, two specific formats for conversation postings provide functionality for polls and events which support commonly used use cases such as event planning and consensus based decision making.

The vast amount of content that can be generated by all of the available mechanisms, especially given the open nature of the platform, can make finding the right information daunting for both the inexperienced as well as veteran Yammer user. In order to minimize this factor and provide an efficient user experience, Yammer provides a consolidated search that is available on each page and searches all postings, files, people and groups within the current network. Search results are provided instantly as the terms are entered as well as in a more detailed format once the search is executed. Tools are also available to narrow the search by date and limit its scope to a single group.

Consuming and Creating Content

Today's users are accustomed to accessing relevant content at the time and place of their choosing and using a large variety of tools and devices. For Yammer to deliver on the promise of rapid engagement and seamless collaboration, it must support those habits.

Yammer's primary client platform is a web browser. When using the platform through a browser, all of the features are available and the experience is intuitive and rich. All recent versions of Microsoft Internet Explorer, Mozilla Firefox, Google Chrome and Apple's Safari are supported providing a similar experience across most commonly used browsers and operating systems. The browser interface can be customized to each organization in an enterprise deployment by selecting corporate color schemes and logos that will appear on each page.

Content is also accessible via applications for mobile devices running iOS, Android or Windows Phone as well as a Windows 8 Modern application. The feature set available in each of these application is specific to the endpoint OS and varies from one platform and another. While consumption of basic content is available with all applications, content creation or work with more complex content types is currently best done with the full browser based application.

For users that only occasionally interact with Yammer and do not have a need for a custom interface, Yammer support basic content consumption and creation via email. Users can post to a group by replying to the Yammer notification emails for that group or using the group's Yammer email address (for example engineering+companyabc.com@yammer.com). While this solution only supports basic content and is far from elegant, it is very easy to use and simplifies engagement. As a result, email based content is a great fit for multiple use cases in most organizations.

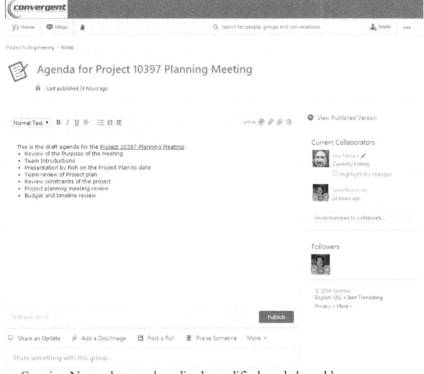

Creating Notes that can be edited, modified, and shared by many users

In addition to the browser and platform specific clients, Yammer provides additional interfaces for specific use cases and needs. First, for a more seamless interaction when working on a primary desktop, Yammer Desktop Notifier is a small Windows application that runs in the background and provides notifications for new relevant content. Second, browser extensions for Google Chrome and Internet Explorer are available to facilitate sharing content directly from a web page. The Internet Explorer extension is built into Windows 8 as a Share Charm while the Google Chrome extension is a download that's available from Yammer's client download site.

The large number of available clients and access methods mirrors the overall philosophy of the Yammer platform which allows users to control the content that they see as they choose to engage or disengage from various groups, audiences or other members. The granular control provided by the combination of access methods and content selection gives user the right tools to make sure that they have access to all relevant data efficiently and seamlessly.

Where Does Yammer Fit In?

Yammer joins an Office 365 product line with several other platforms and products, most of which are geared at collaboration and communication. Understanding Yammer's strengths and weaknesses relative to the rest of the Office 365 offerings allows an organization to identify ideal use cases for Yammer and improve the chances for a successful implementation. Exchange Online, SharePoint Online and Lync Online are all collaboration platforms that offer solutions in a variety of functional areas. Understanding the capabilities of these platform is also a key factor in correctly positioning Yammer within an organization's IT strategy.

Yammer and Exchange

One of the most immediate and intuitive use cases for Yammer is to replace email communication. Yammer brings to the table several fundamental changes that can greatly enhance email as a communication method in specific cases. The first and most fundamental shift is that Yammer strives to make information visible to as many people as need to see it and to do so allows users to control what content they see by joining groups, networks or following other members. For a non-participant to join an email conversation, they must be invited by someone on the thread, in order to join a Yammer discussion, one only has to search for a topic.

One of key features, therefore, to allow people to discover content that is relevant to them is the global search engine that can be used to discover discussions and groups covering topics that are of interest. While it is very easy to include or invite someone into a Yammer discussion or group, the game changer is that users can seek out the conversation without knowing who is already involved in it or waiting for approval or an invitation.

Users who join a topic of discussion already in progress benefit greatly from the historical record of the conversation that is part of the group or network. The historical content provides the full context and details of the topic to date and makes it much easier for someone to catch up on the topic. This capability is of great benefit to team members such as managers or liaisons to other department who may only need occasional visibility into many topics.

There are also use cases typically served by Public Folders that Yammer is well suited for. A common one is the creation of bulletin boards. Yammer announcements and postings to the all company group or specially created groups can address a variety of needs in the areas of bulletin boards and announcements.

While Yammer is well suited to augment or improve upon email and Exchange Online in specific use cases, it is not intended to or well suited for replacing emails as a company's core communication tool. Exchange Online is still the workhorse of communication and collaboration and its versatility, maturity and prevalence ensure that it will continue to be so for the foreseeable future. However, use cases that can benefit from transparency, dynamic membership and informal collaboration are often better served by Yammer.

It's Time for a Chat

Lync Online is the Office 365 product offering focused on real time collaboration, whether via chat, voice or video. The collaboration is primarily internal and the tool is very well integrated into the user's environment with multiple platform clients and strong integration with Outlook. Lync has minimal integration with Yammer and while they are similar in function, there is very little overlap, primarily created by Yammer's chat feature which is text only and much more limited than Lync.

The result is that Lync and Yammer co-exist very well together with users typically bypassing the Yammer chat feature in favor of using Lync for all real time communication needs and Yammer for its strengths around discussions with historical records, strong search and user controlled audiences/groups. That said, there are sometimes special use cases that prefer the Yammer chat function, such as when a group of users doesn't have access to Lync or operates primarily in a browser environment.

SharePoint or Yammer

SharePoint Online has much more in common with Yammer than any of the other Office 365 offerings. It provides parallel functionality in almost every feature of Yammer including: discussion threads, file management, feed based presentation and flexible audience configuration. However, the core differences between the products tend to create a clear differentiation between the use cases for each platform.

The core differences, as with Exchange Online, revolve around the openness of Yammer's content model. A non-participant can control the content they are working with rather than relying on an administrator to grant them access. Sharing content with external collaborators without creating them accounts on your system is another area where the open Yammer model presents an advantage. And of course, the availability of a wide base of client software for Yammer content management provides an advantage over SharePoint.

SharePoint's strengths are in the areas of file management and working with structured data. Yammer's file capabilities are very basic and unlikely to fulfill the needs of an organization, especially one with compliance or regulatory requirements. The feature set of SharePoint is also built around the efficient management and retrieval of structured data within lists and libraries. This feature set, collectively known as content management is not served by Yammer at all.

In the feature areas of significant overlap, such as discussion boards and newsfeeds, the open and collaborative nature of Yammer as well as the ease of access to the data gives the Yammer platform a significant edge. Luckily, this is a not an 'either or' choice. As the next section will highlight, there are options to get the best of both worlds when working with SharePoint Online and Yammer.

Better together - Yammer and SharePoint

Two tools that are so powerful and complement each other like Yammer and SharePoint require mechanisms to interoperate and leverage each other's strengths. With SharePoint Online and Yammer, Microsoft provides sophisticated integration options that satisfy a large number of use cases. First and foremost, the one SharePoint feature that is fully replaced by Yammer is newsfeeds. With the integration of Yammer into Office 365, a single option changes the feed based feature set available in SharePoint from the native newsfeed capability to Yammer. This allows users to quickly engage with the Yammer feature set for the same use cases that newsfeed supported.

For a more planned and seamless integration, Microsoft has released the Yammer app for SharePoint. This app allows the page creator or editor to embed a Yammer feed into a SharePoint page supporting many common scenarios that leveraging Yammer for its strengths around conversations and discussions while using SharePoint as the repository for documents and structured data. The final piece of the integration plan has not been released as of the writing of this book but has been announced and is expected imminently. The final piece involves the integration of Yammer with Office 365 as a whole and includes the integration of authentication for Yammer with Office 365. This will allow not only single sign on for Yammer but also inclusion of Yammer feeds directly on the Office 365 portal screen.

Thoughts and Questions

- Where in your organization do you see Enterprise Social Networking improve how users communicate and get their jobs done?
- Who in your organization or in a specific department would be the best evangelist to start the Yammer adoption in the organization?
- In your organization, will Yammer be best leveraged as a feedback mechanism? To replace old Exchange public folders? To supplement existing SharePoint functionality?

17 MICROSOFT OFFICE IN OFFICE 365

Microsoft Office is Microsoft Office, many users take for granted what has become the default standard in office productivity tools in enterprises. Users leverage the capabilities of 4 key Microsoft Office components for word processing (Microsoft Word), spreadsheets (Microsoft Excel), presentations (Microsoft PowerPoint), and email access (Microsoft Outlook).

Using the Full Office Client for Windows

Office 365 supports virtually any version of Microsoft Office as long as the version of Office can read the file formats of the content being stored and shared in Office 365. Microsoft has a requirement of Outlook 2007 SP2 or higher for Outlook to leverage the capabilities in Outlook for failover of email servers between sites, built in encryption between Outlook and Office 365, and for legacy public folder access for organizations still using public folders.

However for Word, Excel, and PowerPoint, content stored in Office 365 is merely just the standard document formats. Microsoft does not convert the content to any special file format when content is saved in Office 365. DOC files, XLS files, PPT files, DOCX files, XLSX files, PPTX files are all saved in their native format. So as long as a version of Office app can access the file format, it can be used with Office 365.

Obviously Microsoft has stated versions they officially support, and as such, keeping to a supported version ensures your users will get assistance if they have any problems with Office 365. The key though is that Microsoft Office 365 doesn't convert documents and file formats, so that content saved in Office 365 can still be attached to emails and shared with other Microsoft Office users.

Using the Full Office Client for Macs

Apple Mac users are also required to use an up to date version of Outlook 2011 for Mac to securely access email messages, however Mac users can also open and save files in Word for Mac, Excel for Mac, or PowerPoint for Mac just as they've done for years. File formats remain the same across various Office versions, although again, Microsoft's official support is for Office 2011 for Mac or more current.

Leveraging Office Web Apps for Browser-based Users

What may be new for many users is what Microsoft provides in Office 365 for users who want to open, access, and even EDIT Office content right from a browser. If the user is working from a system that doesn't have Microsoft Office installed, or potentially the copy of Office is an older 2003 edition that didn't support opening of the DOCX format Word files, the built in Office Web Apps to Office 365 is a great solution.

Office Web Apps runs from any modern browser and has the most common editing features built in to the Web app. Users can open content, change fonts, change styles, add colors and formatting, perform spellchecks, insert comments, print, and save content among other features.

Editing a Word Document Straight from a Browser Session

Office Web Apps may not be the best tool for someone who uses the over 1500 features in Word, Excel, or PowerPoint on a regular basis, however for the user who simply wants to change a few words, make a couple structure edits to a document, the Office Web App functionality works extremely well for those purposes.

Installing Microsoft Office Using Click-to-Run Installation

To simplify the distribution of Office 2013 for users, Microsoft has included what they call the "Click-to-Run installation" of Office. Instead of an organization having to burn and distribute DVDs of software code, users can simply go to the Microsoft Office 365 website and click to install Office 2013 (for Windows systems) and Office 2011 (for Apple Mac systems) straight to their systems.

The code is streamed to the user's system and installs on the system. Office 365 keeps track of the systems that the user has installed the software to, and a user's system must communicate back to Microsoft at least every 30-days to keep the license active. If the user's system does not communicate up to Office 365 after 30-days, the software goes into a "reduced functionality mode" and the user is informed to make sure to connect to the Internet to re-instate full functionality. This also helps an organization manage software licenses such as if a user installs Office on a couple personal systems and then leaves the organization, the user's Office 365 account is disabled or eliminated, and as such, the user's copies of Office no longer become fully usable.

Licensing Office for Office 365 Users

Microsoft has various versions of Office 365 with some of the Office 365 licenses include the Microsoft Office client. When an organization purchases an Office 365 license that includes Office, the user can install up to 5 copies of Office on various systems. The systems can be Windows-based systems and/or Apple Mac-based systems. Microsoft has great flexibility in the support of different platforms as well as supports the fact that most users these days have work-based systems, home systems, laptops systems, and tablets that all tie to the single user, and thus the Office license is portable to support all of the devices for the user.

Thoughts and Questions

- Do your users for the most part use Microsoft Office (either Windows or Mac) and are familiar with the Office components?
- Are there times when users may find the Office Web App a quick and easy solution for viewing and lightly editing content?
- Does the option to allow users to click to install Office themselves

simplify the task of I.T. by providing users access to Office code for self installation?

- Will the licensing option of allowing users to install Office on up to 5 of their devices be seen as a benefit for users throughout the enterprise?

18 GETTING STARTED WITH OFFICE 365

After 17 chapters of going through the most common questions about Office 365, what's included, what works, what doesn't work, hopefully you're at a point where you are ready to get started with Office 365. You still don't have to be 100% committed to migrating fully to Office 365, and at that, you can simply choose just one area of Office 365 to migrate to such as just email, or just SharePoint. Microsoft provides a 30-day trial access that allows you to at least see firsthand the features and functions covered in this book.

Setting Up an Office 365 Trial

Microsoft provides a free 30-day trial of Office 365. As the focus of this book is on the Enterprise edition of Office 365, getting an Enterprise trial will allow you to see things like Outlook, OneDrive, SharePoint, and the administrator tools in Office 365 pretty quickly and easily.

To setup an Office 365 trial, do the following:

1. Using your favorite browser, navigate to
   http://office.microsoft.com/en-us/try
2. This page defaults to home users, so click "Try Office for Business" towards the bottom right of the page.
3. Click on "Compare Plans".
4. Click on the "Enterprise" tab on the Compare Office 365 for business page. This page and the previous page compare all of the features available in the various Office 365 for Business plans.

5. Scroll down on the page until you see the "Free trial" link under the Office 365 Enterprise E3 column.

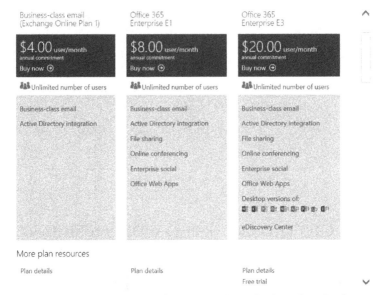

Choosing the Free Trial in the Enterprise E3 Licensing Option

6. Fill out the form to start your free 30-day trial of the Office 365 Enterprise E3 plan

    a. You'll notice the "User ID" section has two components, the first being your username and the second being what they call your "tenant name". In our example we're using "alex" as the username and "o365rocks" as the tenant name, making our final User ID "alex@o365rocks.onmicrosoft.com".

    b. The "Verify your phone number" section is an important security step that allows Microsoft to prevent users from creating an unlimited number of test tenants that never get used. Here you can enter a mobile number or landline number, just make sure to select the "Call me" option if you are entering a number that cannot receive text messages. Click on the "Send text message" or "Call me" button depending on the option you chose for verification.

    c. Once all fields are filled in and you receive your verification code via text message or phone call, click on "Create my Account".

7. Once the account creation process finishes, you will be taken to the "Office 365 Admin Center". You will then be prompted to fill out account recovery information. This is an important step in being able to access your account should you ever forget or lose your password. Enter in an alternate phone number and e-mail address and click "Save and Close" to return to the Admin Center.

8. At this point, you will need to wait for your services to be provisioned before you can start creating mailboxes and using all of the features of Office 365 for Business. You can see the current status of your service provisioning on the "Dashboard" page of the Admin Center under the "Service Overview" section and the "Service Health" tab. Any service that is not ready for you to use will say "Provisioning…" next to it. All others will say "No issues" or report any system-wide issues that could have an effect on users.

Service Health – Checking on Provisioning Status

Getting Familiar with the Office 365 Administration Functions

Once you have the Office 365 tenant setup, you can walk through some of the most common administrative tasks in Office 365. The following is a walkthrough of common administration tasks:

1. Logon to your Office 365 for Business account by navigating to https://portal.microsoftonline.com

2. Using the User ID and password that you created during the trial sign up process, enter it using the username@tenant.onmicrosoft.com format. In our example, it was alex@o365rocks.onmicrosoft.com

3. Creating users is one of the most common tasks in the admin center, start by clicking on the "Users and Groups" tab on the left of the page.

    a. As of now, you'll only see yourself in the list. Create a new user by clicking on the "+" symbol at the top of the list.

    b. Enter details for your new user: First name, last name, display name, and user name (what's going to go in front of @o365rocks.onmicrosoft.com). If you choose to fill out first name and last name, the "display name" property will auto-populate for you. You can add things like job title and phone numbers by expanding "addition details". Click on "next" after this information is filled out.

    c. On the "settings" page you'll be asked if you want to assign any roles to the user. This allows the user you're creating to administer certain or all aspects of the Office 365 for Business account. You're also required to set a location for the user. The location you chose when creating your Office 365 for Business trial will be the first option in the list. Click on "next" after selecting the appropriate options.

    d. This brings us to the "assign licenses" page, which is one of the most important steps in creating a user. Licenses are what actually give users access to the services of Office 365 for Business such as Exchange and Lync. In your trial, you have 25 licenses available for each service in the plan (24 since one is assigned to your user account by default. Select the licenses you want to apply to the users, by default all are selected, then click on "next" when complete.

Configuring Licensing for an Office 365 User

> e. On the "send results" page, you can choose to send the results of the new user account, including the temporary password, to a specified e-mail address. Note that passwords are sent in clear text through e-mail and this may not meet regulatory standards. Select whether or not you want to send the e-mail, then click on "create" to finish the user creation process.

> f. After a quick couple of seconds, you will be presented with the results of your new user, including the username and temporary password to give to your user. Upon signing in to https://portal.microsoftonline.com with these details, your user will be prompted to change their temporary password. Click on "finish" to return to the "Users and Groups" page.

4. One other page you may use frequently is the "Service Settings" tab. On this page you will find very basic options for administering Exchange, SharePoint, and Lync as well as password policies.

Service Settings Options in Office 365

Getting Familiar with the Exchange Administration Functions

As email is one of the key things organizations migrates to Office 365 for, this section goes through the most common Exchange Administration tasks in Office 365. The tasks are as follows:

1. Get to the Exchange Admin Center by click on the "Admin" button at the top right of the Office 365 Admin Center page, then selecting "Exchange" from the list. The default page is the "recipients" tab. Here you can manage options for your user mailboxes, distribution groups, resource mailboxes, shared mailboxes, contacts, and mailbox migrations.

Exchange Admin Center in Office 365

2. To create a distribution group, click on the "groups" tab.

    a. Click on the drop down arrow next to the "+" button to select from a distribution group, a security group, and a dynamic distribution group. These steps will walk you through creating a distribution group.

    b. A window will pop up with options for the new distribution group. Fill out the "Display name" and "Alias". The alias will be the part of the e-mail address in front of "@TenantName.onmicrosoft.com". In our example it is "o365help" for the alias, making the address of the distribution group "o365help@o365rocks.onmicrosoft.com". You can fill out a description for the group as well. Select an owner or owners for the group, it will default to the person creating the group. To add members to the group, click on the "+" under the "Members" options and select users to be in the group. By default, owners of the group are added as members but this is not reflected in the members list.

    c. Select any of the other available options and then click on "save" once you are finished.

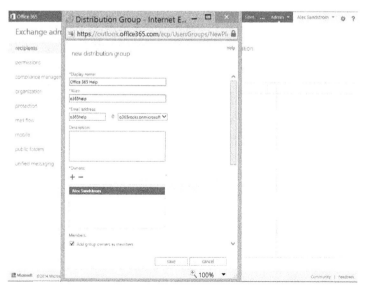

Managing Distribution Groups in Office 365

3. Granting administrative permissions, or "admin roles" as they are called in Office 365, is another common task. Click on the "permissions" tab on the left, this will put you at the "admin roles" page by default.

 a. To assign an admin role to a user, double-click on the admin role that you wish to add a user to. We'll use the "Help Desk" role in our example. This allows a user to reset the password of other users, view all attributes of users, and change the options of users that the users themselves can change. Another common role group is "Organization Management". This role group allows a user to administer all aspects of the Exchange organization in Office 365, so be careful with who you assign it to.

 b. Once in the role group options, scroll down to the "Members" section and click on the "+" to add a user to the group, then click on "save" once you are done. Note that you can also add an entire "security group" to a role group to assign permissions, not just individual users.

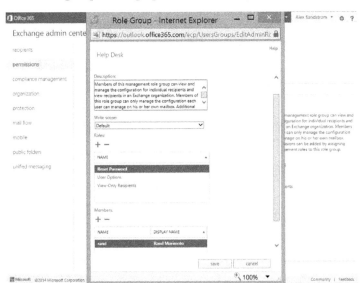

Establishing Administrative Roles in Office 365

4. Performing a message trace allows you to track messages sent and received in your organization. Common use cases are users wanting to verify if a message they sent went through and was received

inside the organization, or the business wanting to see if a user sent a particular message outside of the organization that maybe they shouldn't have. Click on the "mail flow" tab on the left side, then click on the "message trace" tab at the top to start a new trace.

a. Once the message trace page loads, you will be presented with many different criteria to search by: date range (time zone, start date/time, and end date/time appear if you select "Custom" for the data range), delivery status, message ID, sender, and recipient. You can select multiple users or distribution groups for both sender and recipient.

b. Once you have filled out the criteria to search for, click on the "search" button at the bottom to begin the trace. A new window will pop up with the results of the trace, once you are done, you can click on "close".

Message Tracing in Office 365

c. To view previous traces or traces that are still running (this happens often if you are running a broad search in a large organization with a lot of mail flow), you can click on "View pending or completed traces" at the top of "message trace" page.

Getting Familiar with the Basic Functions of Outlook Web App

Office 365 provides the ability for users to access their email either through the full Outlook client (2007, 2010, 2013, Mac 2011) or through a browser interface. The Outlook Web App is the browser interface that users can access their email, calendar appointments, and contacts from virtually anywhere. Some of the basic steps to using Outlook Web App:

1. There are two ways to access Outlook Web App:

    a. If you are not already logged in to Office 365, navigate to https://outlook.office365.com and sign in using the Office 365 User ID and password that you created during sign up.

    b. If you are already logged in to Office 365, simply click on the "Outlook" link up at the top of any Office 365 page.

2. As mentioned earlier in the book, the experience in Outlook Web App is very similar to the Windows Outlook application: mailbox folders on the left, list of conversation in the middle, and the preview pane on the right. The first thing you will probably want to do is compose and send an e-mail.

    a. Click on "new mail" up in the top left corner of the page.

    b. Your new e-mail will appear in the preview pane, with all of the fields you would expect: To, Cc, Subject, and the message body with formatting options. You can click on "To" or "Cc" to select recipients from your address book (once the address book comes up, clicking on ">>" will expand the recipient options and allow you to select from the organization's directory as well).

    c. Along the top of the new mail pane, you have buttons to send, discard, and insert attachments. By clicking the "…" button more options appear such as saving as a draft, showing Bcc, or setting importance.

    d. Compose a message and click the send button.

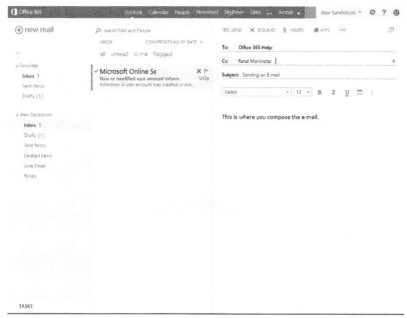

Composing an Email Message in Office 365

3. Calendaring in Outlook Web App is just as intuitive and feature-rich as the e-mailing experience. To open the calendar, click on the "Calendar" link up at the top of any Office 365 page.

   a. The calendar will default to displaying the events for the current day. The layout is, again, very similar to the Windows Outlook application: a small month-view and a list of all of your available calendars on the left, a larger calendar view for the month (default), week, work week, or day in the middle, and details of the selected day on the right. To change the middle view, select "day", "work week", "week", or "month" in the top right corner of the page. You can also change the current month along the top middle of the page.

   b. Create a new calendar event by clicking on "new event" in the top left corner of the page.

   c. Your new event window will pop up and you'll be presented with all of the same fields as you would in Outlook: Event name, location (with ability to select a room mailbox, attendees (if creating a meeting), start date and time, duration (instead of an end date and time, reminder, repeat options, and event details with formatting options.

d. Along the top of the pop up pane you have buttons to send or save if a personal appointment, discard, and view scheduling assistant. By clicking on the "…" button options appear to insert an attachment or picture, and to categorize the event.

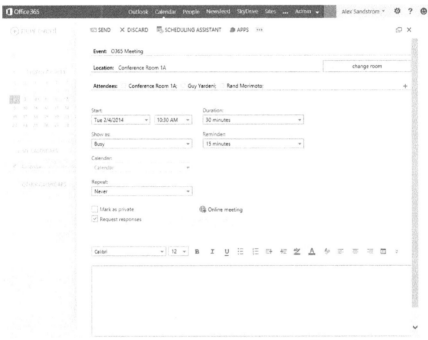

Working with Calendar Appointments in Office 365

e. Fill out all of your event details and click on the send or save button. You'll be taken back to the main calendar view and you should now be able to see your new event.

High Level Punch list for a Migration to Office 365

To end this chapter and this book, I'm going to put together a handful of punch list items to work through as part of the moving forward with Office 365.

- ☐ Confirm that your environment meets the pre-requisites for an Office 365 deployment (specifically version of Outlook supported, version of browsers supported http://www.microsoft.com/en-cb/office365/system-requirements.aspx

- ☐ If you'll be migrating from a previous version of Exchange, make sure Exchange has the appropriate Service Pack needed for migration and co-existence http://technet.microsoft.com/en-us/library/hh534377%28v=exchg.150%29.aspx

- ☐ Perform an Office 365 readiness assessment of the pre-requisites against your environment and update anything that needs to be updated to be Office 365 ready.

- ☐ Setup a 30-day trial of Office 365 (likely Enterprise E3 or E4 that is common for businesses) or onboard your Office 365 tenant subscription that you may have purchased as part of your Microsoft Enterprise Agreement (see your Microsoft Sales representative or Consulting partner for assistance)

- ☐ Setup ADFS and/or DirSync replication to integrate your Active Directory to Office 365

- ☐ Configure your existing Exchange environment (or existing non-Microsoft email environment) to be ready for mail, calendar appointments, contacts, and other data to be migrated into Office 365

- ☐ Move a couple mailboxes to confirm the process works and to uncover any migration experiences that need to be fine-tuned to simplify the process for the rest of the users.

- ☐ Move a handful of additional users to Office 365. Update your migration procedures and work through any problem solving needed

- ☐ Move a pilot group of users that includes users with various versions of Outlook and mobile devices that would be a good sampling of the organization to test experiences across a variety of systems.

- ☐ Schedule and move the balance of users, either in bulk or staged over a period of time.

ABOUT THE AUTHORS

Rand Morimoto, Ph.D., MBA, CISSP, MCITP: Dr Morimoto is the President of Convergent Computing (CCO), a San Francisco Bay Area based strategy and technology consulting firm. CCO helps organizations development and fine tune their technology strategies, and then provide hands-on assistance planning, preparing, implementing, and supporting the technology infrastructures. CCO works with Microsoft and other industry leading hardware and software vendors in early adopter programs, gaining insight and hands-on expertise to the technologies far before they are released to the general public. CCO has had the opportunity to work with Microsoft Office 365 in such early adopter programs allowing experts and Rand to develop tips, tricks, and best practices based on lessons learned.

Guy Yardeni, MCITP, CISSP, MVP: Guy is an accomplished infrastructure architect, author and overall geek for hire. Guy has been working in the IT industry for over 15 years and has extensive experience designing, implementing and supporting enterprise technology solutions. Guy is an expert at connecting business requirements to technology solutions and driving to successful completion the technical details of the effort while maintaining overall goals and vision. Guy maintains a widely read technical blog at www.rdpfiles.com and is a Windows MVP.

www.ingramcontent.com/pod-product-compliance
Lightning Source LLC
Chambersburg PA
CBHW071220050326
40689CB00011B/2384